# COOL careers for girls in Performing Arts

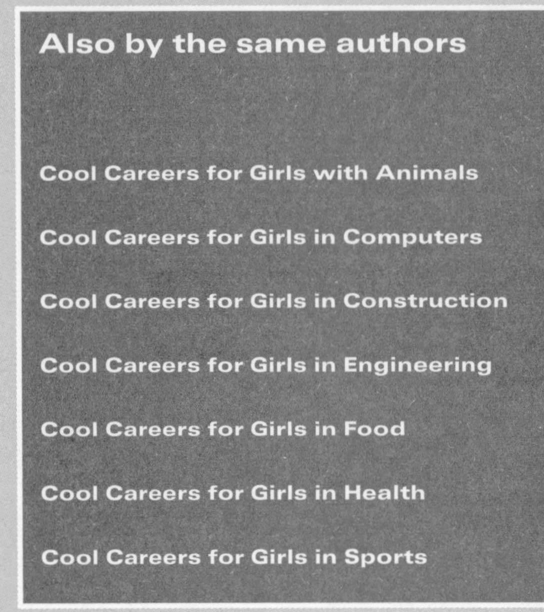


IMPACT PUBLICATIONS

# COOL careers for girls in Performing Arts





CEEL PASTERNAK & LINDA THORNBURG

---

**Library of Congress Data**

Pasternak, Ceel, 1932-
Cool careers for girls in performing arts / Ceel Pasternak & Linda Thornburg.
p. cm.
Includes bibliographical references
ISBN 1-57023-136-2 (hbk.)—ISBN 1-57023-132-X (pbk.)
LC 00022460

---

**Publisher:** For information on Impact Publications, including current and forthcoming publications, authors, press kits, bookstore, and submission requirements, visit Impact's Web site: www.impactpublications.com

**Publicity/Rights:** For information on publicity, author interviews, and subsidiary rights, contact the Public Relations and Marketing Department: Tel. 703/361-7300 or Fax 703/335-9486.

**Sales/Distribution**: All paperback bookstore sales are handled through Impact's trade distributor: National Book Network, 15200 NBN Way, Blue Ridge Summit, PA 17214, Tel. 1-800-462-6420. All other sales and distribution inquiries should be directed to the publisher: Sales Department, IMPACT PUBLICATIONS, 9104-N Manassas Dr., Manassas Park, VA 20111-5211, Tel. 703/361-7300, Fax 703/335-9486, or E-mail: coolcareers@impactpublications.com

Book design by Guenet Abraham
Desktopped by C. M. Grafik

# Contents

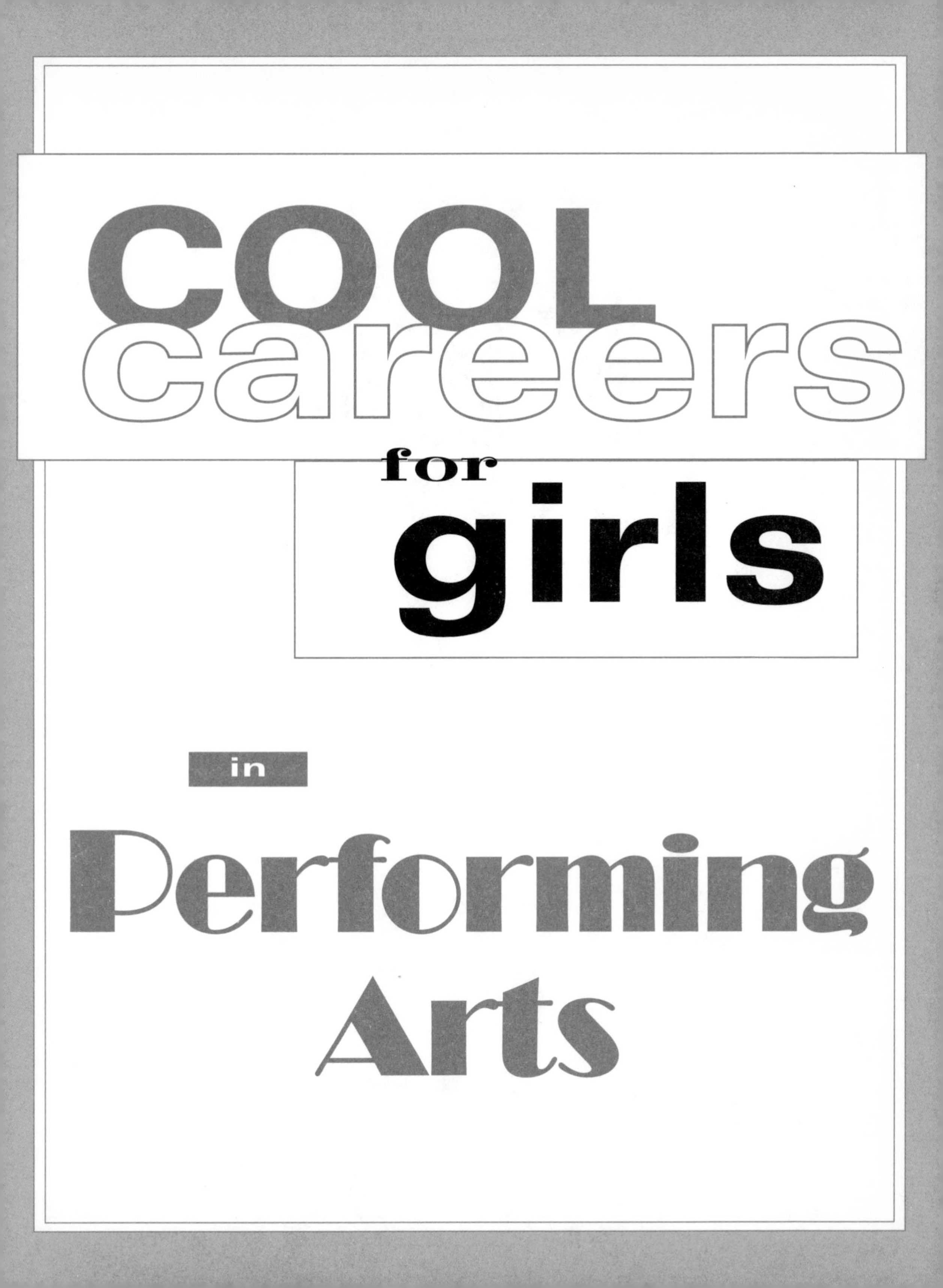
COOL
careers
for
girls
in
Performing
Arts

*Dedicated, with appreciation, to performing artists and to inspired young people who love to perform.*

## A Special Introduction by Jeri Goldstein

**Author of *How To Be Your Own Booking Agent And Save Thousands Of Dollars;***
**President of The New Music Times, Inc., since 1976, currently focusing on publishing, artist career development seminars, and consulting.**

**In William Shakespeare's day, women were not even allowed to act the role of a woman on stage—boys and young men whose voices had not yet changed acted the female parts, dressed in appropriate costumes. Those days are long gone.**

Do you want to be a rock star or a concert pianist? Perhaps you dream of being a dancer in a Broadway show or even of having your own television series. Maybe you have fantasized about becoming a movie star. Or, perhaps playing cello in the symphony or playing violin in a string quartet is more your style. You may be interested in the music itself and would rather conduct an orchestra instead. Have you ever thought that it would be fun to be the lead singer in your own band and play your songs for audiences all over the country? You might even think about sharing your love of your performance art with children, performing for school assembly programs, or doing workshops in classrooms. The possibilities for a career in the performing arts are endless, with exciting opportunities for women in all areas of the entertainment field.

Make no mistake, there is a great deal of hard work that goes into developing a successful performing arts career. But, as many working professional performing artists have told me, (and I've booked national and international tours for artists performing in country, folk, gospel, bluegrass, contemporary, classical, and children's music and also booked tours for theater and dance) all of the work is worth the effort because their love and passion for their art form motivates them every day.

In most performers, that passion is developed early in their lives. As a former booking agent and artist's manager, I worked with a variety of performing artists whose passion for their art form was born at a very young age. They developed their talent as they grew up by taking lessons, finding mentors, and learning as much as possible about their art and how to perfect their talent. They decided to make their art their career much later in life and then found it necessary to learn about their specific industry so they could earn a living.

As you will read in the following pages, each woman featured is passionate about her performing career. Each continues to raise her level of talent so she may excel within her chosen field. Each must conduct the business of her art in order to maintain her place within the industry. Competition is stiff in the performing arts, with many talented individuals hoping to be the one among the many recognized as having something unique and interesting to say through their performance. A performing arts career demands excellence and perseverance.

In today's entertainment industry, many performers have a rare opportunity to create their own destiny by using the technology available to market themselves. Singer/songwriter Ani DiFranco redefined success as a recording artist by establishing her own record label, rather than signing a contract with one of the major recording companies. She created a loyal following for her unique style of music and found a way of doing business on her own terms. Her methods are being copied by many new performers all over the world and are envied by many major labels.

Many artists are finding new audiences for their performances and are creating their own unique niche markets. Others are following more traditional routes by finding careers in established theater and dance companies or orchestras. Interestingly, the performing arts may be unique among career choices in that a totally new performance style or approach can become popular seemingly overnight. An individual performer can gain widespread popularity in what seems to be an instant within some forms of the popular performing arts. At the same time, many artists design a completely satisfying yet less glamorous performing arts career.

No matter what level of success a performer achieves, no matter how quickly her rise to fame may seem, a career in the performing arts takes these four traits—a commitment to developing your talent, a passion for your art form, a deep love for sharing your talent with an audience, and an understanding of the industry in which your specific field exists. Any woman gifted with those traits has many opportunities to find or create a career in the performing arts.

### Discover if a Performing Arts Career is for You

When a girl displays the slightest talent or exhibits some interest in one form of performance or another, she is often encouraged to pursue that talent with after-school lessons. In school, she joins the drama club, the orchestra, marching band, or chorus. For many girls, an interest in lessons fades, band practice interferes with more interesting aspects of growing up, and rehearsal sessions are replaced with team sports, cheerleading, and general socializing. However, for some girls, the gift for a specific performing art form grows into such a passion that they decide to nurture their talent to the point where it might become a career. For those career-bound performing artists there exist many courses of study to help young artists to make their dream to perform a lifetime reality.

Along with private lessons, in-school introductory courses, and after-school activities in the performing arts, there are numerous schools and camps all over the world specializing in specific fields of the arts. For example, the Walden School in New Hampshire concentrates on music composition during their summer camp. The Harrad Institute in Florida has courses in music, dance, and theater. The High School of the Performing Arts in New York City became famous during the 70s when it was featured in the movie *Fame*. Pop artist and singer / songwriter Janis Ian attended that high school. She had a hit record while still in her teens.

There are competitions, showcases, conferences, college level music, theater and dance programs, and private studios that are taught by master craftspeople. The Actors Studio in New York City is just one example.

As a student of the performing arts, a talented artist is not only expected to constantly improve her talent by taking classes, she must also compete for audition openings, showcase slots, and performance dates in order to find and expand her audience and move her career to the next level. In the pages of this book, you will discover how these women performers met and continue to meet these challenges.

## How To Use This Book

As you read each woman's story, you'll find a checklist with some clues about what type of person would be good in the particular area profiled. You'll get ideas of what a typical day is like and what makes the hard work worthwhile to the performer. There is information about what salary you might expect to earn as you start out and as you grow.

The final chapter, Getting Started on Your Own Career Path, gives you some advice from the women on what to do now. You'll find recommendations on books to read and a list of organizations to contact for information.

# Jane Beard

Jane Beard

**Repertory Company,** Round House Theater, Silver Spring, Maryland

Member of Screen Actors Guild, Actor's Equity Union, and American Federation of Television and Radio Actors

Major in political science

# Screen and Stage Actress

## Her Curiosity Brings Characters to Life

Jane Beard is in the midst of preparing for three acting roles this year as a member of the Round House Theater Repertory Company in Silver Spring, Maryland. In the first acting role, she plays a 39-year-old, unmarried woman who lives with her mother and three adult siblings. Jane's character is upset when her mother marries again, and she tries to seduce her mother's husband. "It would probably be good for this character to be a little overweight," Jane says. In the second play, she will be a prostitute with a heart of gold, who ends up getting involved in solving a murder that happened 20 years ago. "This character needs to be in good shape, so I will work with a trainer to

**ACTOR:** Salaries are usually low except for the best known performers. That is why actors take many different jobs that use their talents. They also do part-time work in nonrelated fields.

*Earnings for actors who are members of a union and sign a union contract:*
**BROADWAY ACTORS** earn a minimum of $1,000 per week; Off Broadway actors earn from $380 to $650 per week. On tour, the actors earn an additional $100 a day.
**MOTION PICTURE AND TELEVISION ACTORS** earn $500 to $1,750 for a 5-day week. Extras earn a minimum of $100 a day. According to individual contracts, actors get paid additional money (called residuals) when the TV show or film is rerun; film actors sometimes negotiate a percentage of the profits.

Source: *Career Information Center* (7th ed.). (1999). Macmillan

prepare for her part." In the third, she will portray two people, a suburban Connecticut housewife whose alcoholic brother has just died and the character's mother.

"I know about a year in advance what roles I will be doing at Round House. The theater chooses a year's worth of plays in late February. From December through February, we read scripts and try to figure out which works would be best to produce. I don't think just about the roles I would like during this time; I think about what is best for the theater. Then if I get to act in them, so much the better."

To prepare for her roles once they are assigned, Jane collects images to fit her characters. "I start listening actively for what kind of music feels right for this character. It won't necessarily be music the character has heard, just music that feels like what this character would be attracted to, or that represents this character somehow. I look for what kind of books this person might read, or what color they might wear. Even if I don't get to wear that color in the play it helps to keep collecting images to fit the person. I'm constantly thinking about these characters."

One advantage to acting in the repertory company is that the company's artistic director sometimes chooses plays with Jane in mind. Another advantage is that Jane is working with the same actors over time. They all get to know each other and often give their best performances because of the chemistry between them. Jane has a special acting partner. They play husband and wife, sis-

Acts in regional theater, day job as fund raiser

Gets first work in a commercial

Goes to acting full-time

ter and brother, and other combinations. "I am so lucky to have him. We take an interest in each other's careers. Things happen between us on stage that wouldn't happen between other actors. The people's opinions I value most are my acting partner, my husband, and my artistic director. People I know, who have known my work over time and are able to give me the best feedback, see what I'm trying to achieve."

## Being Somebody Different

Jane acted in her first play in the seventh grade. "I was better than anybody else, and I thought acting was something I could really be good at. I liked being somebody different." But even though she was a good actress from the time she was 12, it took Jane a long time to develop an acting career.

Before she figured out how to make a full-time career out of acting, Jane tried working as a pollster for a consumer products research company and for a consultant to the Democratic Party. Then she worked as a fundraiser for a women's rights organization. Eventually she found her way into full-time acting.

"When I graduated from college, there was a woman in the theater department who had her own theater and she kept calling me and saying 'Why don't you come do this role?' I kept working in the theater in my spare time, but I continued to work day jobs. I kept seeing people around me who didn't have day jobs and were making their living doing commer-

cials and voice-overs, and I kept thinking. I should try that. But I still wasn't sure about leaving my day job. I had to have health insurance. You couldn't join the stage actor's union, Equity, unless you had worked at a certain level in theater. This is one way actors get health insurance. But you could join the American Federation of Radio and Television Artists, another actor's union, so I did that. Right after I joined, I was called to audition for a commercial. It was a Folger's Coffee commercial, and I got the job, even though I had never auditioned for commercials before. As a result, I earned enough money to get health insurance for two years. (The union pays your health insurance if you work enough.) Now, health insurance wasn't a concern anymore. I quit my day job and thought, I'll see if I can make enough money to do this for a living. And I have. I've been working

**What is cool about film is that it is so close up that you can tell things without words. In the theater, more words are required.**

as an actress for ten years now, and I work all the time."

Jane says what she needed was the confidence that she could support herself as a responsible adult and be an actress at the same time. "It wasn't that I really needed the health insurance. It was just my excuse for not taking that risk. In the theater there are so many people who exercise an excuse for not doing things—not going to auditions, not putting themselves forward. They put barriers between themselves and success because they don't want to experience failure. One of the things that finally helped me was meeting my present husband, Jeffrey Davis. He was the first person I was really close to who said, 'You are wonderful at this. You ought to be doing it.' My teachers had always told me that, but it's different when it comes from someone you are close to."

## Hollywood and the Movies

Besides acting at Round House Theater, Jane is busy working in Holly-

## CAREER CHECKLIST

### You'll like this job if you ...

- Have a great imagination
- Like to figure out what makes people tick
- Can perform in front of an audience
- Will read lots of plays and attend theater to learn
- Are willing to take risks to develop your career
- Can do lots of different types of acting to make a living

wood films, television, commercials, industrial and training films for the federal government and corporations, and doing voice-overs for commercials, telephone recordings, and the Internet. Her film work includes parts in *Guarding Tess*, with Nicholas Cage and Shirley McLaine, and *Silent Fall*, with Richard Dreyfus. "When I was doing *Guarding Tess*, I had to drop out of a play at Theatre of the First Amendment for a little more than 3 weeks."

In *Silent Fall*, a movie about an autistic child who sees his parents murdered, Jane plays a neighbor who takes care of the child. "It took three days to do the shooting for my part in this. An understudy in the theater went on for me. This is really a nice thing, and Round House is the only theater in town that will let you do that. In the *Silent Fall* scene there are kids, and strict rules govern how long kids can work. So I worked by myself for part of the time, looking at blockings. All directors are different, but this particular one paid attention to me, as opposed to just the stars. We explored the relationship between my character and the dead parents and what it would be like to have the kid in the house. Then lots of people threw food at me for the one scene that made it past the cutting room floor and into the movie. (The autistic child throws a plate of food at Jane in the movie.)

"Film is fun but it gets grueling. Acting on camera has taught me to be ruthlessly specific in my choices. Instead of being mad, I have to know exactly why I am mad and what the person I am mad at can do to fix it. That benefits the way I act on stage too. You find odd things by being specific. For example, the character I am working on now for Round House is trying to seduce her mother's new husband, but is mostly telling herself she wants to get rid of him. The way I will use certain words and props depends on what I believe at each moment as that character. If my mother's husband takes a step toward me, I have

**I don't read reviews. Haven't for years. The people whose opinions I value most are my acting partner, my husband, and the artistic director. If you're acting for the reviews, you're in the wrong business.**

to show that maybe I like it because I could get what I want, but I'm also afraid of that. That's the game of it, the fun of it. How do you solve the puzzles and problems of being that character? Often there are directors who will say, pick up this piece of furniture at this point, or walk over here on this line. I don't like that. This comes from directors who don't trust actors and think only their vision is important."

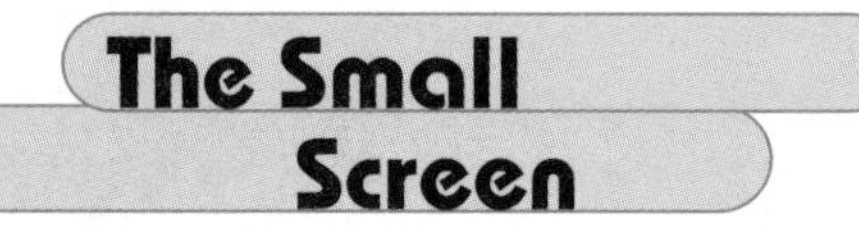

## The Small Screen

Jane has acted on the television shows *Homicide*, *Unsolved Mysteries*, and *America's Most Wanted*. "Television is fast. They do in two weeks what it would take a film director six weeks to do. You just study it, walk through it, and shoot. Any homework you need to do, you better have done way before you get there. You probably will not talk to the people in your scene, you just show up and do it. One thing that is different from the stage is that you have to do the same thing in exactly the same way for a number of different takes—anywhere from 2 to 50. The camera will be shooting from different angles, and then they will be editing all these takes together, so if you are in a different place or doing things differently, it may be noticeable."

"What's great about television and film is that they pay what are called residuals. You can work for three weeks and keep getting paid for five years if the show is still shown. What I love about the theater is the rehearsal part of it, which you don't really get in film or television. That's when you know you are really creating something. It's only recently that I've come to see that the audience is also a part of it. They make it different every night."

## Wednesday Matinees

Jane grew up in Princeton, New Jersey. "As a kid I was pretty serious and willful. I thought I was going to end up as a lawyer. I went to the theater in

New York a lot. Every Wednesday at noon, we would get out of school so the teachers could do their preparatory work. Wednesday is matinee day in New York. A bunch of us would leave school, take the train into New York, go see a play, and come home at 7:00 p.m. I acted every chance I could in high school. When I went to see *A Child's Play* in New York, I waited until the stage manager came out and asked, 'what do I have to do to be this?' He said, 'see as much theater as you can.'"

"In a town near where I grew up there was a really good repertory company called McCarter Theater, and I ushered for everything. The theater also had a creative program for youth, and I took classes in summer and during school. Acting was easy for me. I would work hard in school, work hard taking care of my brothers and sisters as the oldest of four, but acting was just fun. I was so serious, though, that I would usually get cast in the most serious roles. It took me years to realize I could do comedy, which I am now appreciated for. I also read every play I could get my hands on in high school."

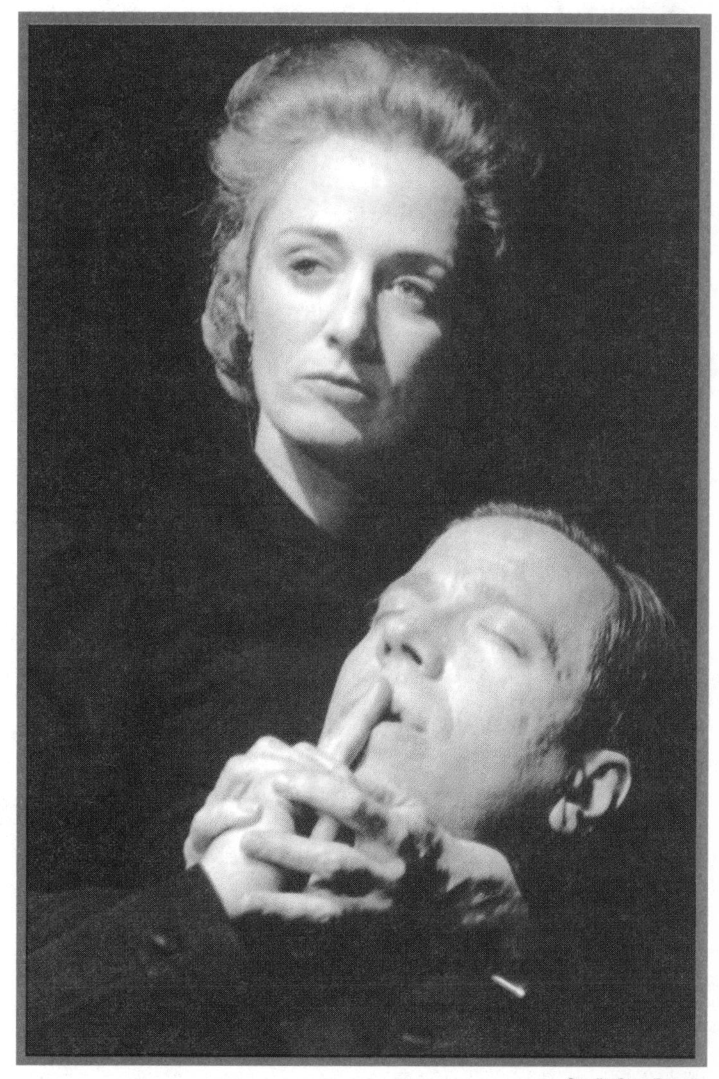

Credit: Stan Barouh

Jane's parents didn't want her to study theater in college because they didn't think it would prepare her for any type of stable work. She changed her major seven times in college—George Washington University in Washington, DC—because she really wanted to act, even though she thought she shouldn't. She finally ended up taking lots of political science. Halfway through college, she took a break and went back home to work for Gallup Polls. "I totally loved it for the same reason that I love theater. You could go into these different worlds. I would get back a survey and wouldn't know the answers to the questions until I tabulated all the responses. Looking at the responses, I'd say, well, if a family makes under $25,000 per year, it's a good bet that they are going to feel this way about this product. Then you would make up reasons and go test for them. Polling and acting are two jobs that are good for curious people."

When she returned to school, Jane continued to act and switched her major to drama. She had enough credits to graduate faster that way, and now she was paying for her own education.

## Stage Fright

About that time, Jane developed stage fright. Everyone she was close

**Even when you have an agent, you have to tell them, "You know, there is this play coming up and I would be good in this role."**

to, including a boyfriend she later married, said she shouldn't be an actress. But when she got out of school she started acting again, and the more she acted, the more she loved it. She eventually divorced her first husband and married Jeffrey, who has always supported her love of acting. The couple has three children, and two of them also love the theater. "I would encourage my kids to go into it if that's what they really want to do. My mother's father was a vaudeville performer, but I never really thought of him as an actor. When my mother was dying she told me she had always wanted me to be an actress; I just didn't know it at the time."

Jane has started a new sideline. She coaches people to help them understand why people around them behave certain ways. Often there are issues that parallel the theater work I'm doing. It keeps me in touch with what people are thinking and helps me exercise the part of my brain that is curious. Why would this be, and not this, I can ask myself. Actors have to know these things about real people."

## GROUNDBREAKERS

### First Lady of American Theater

Helen Hayes (1901-1993), the first lady of American theater, played Queen Victoria in Victoria Regina, which toured 47 cities in the mid 1930s. She made her stage debut at the age of five in a 1900 drama called The Royal Family and much later played Queen Mary in Mary of Scotland. In 1957, she played the Russian princess Anastasia in the film of the same name. Hayes' legendary talent got her some cameo roles in other films, but she will be best remembered for her stage acting. She characterized herself as "The Great White Goddess of the American Stage," and "The Holy Cow." She continued making films in her later years, and also starred in several Disney films (Herbie Rides Again).

Source: Women's History Project

# Tracey Wright

Tracey Wright

**Master Sergeant,** Air Force Band, Bolling Air Force Base, Washington, DC

# Singer, Military Service

## Jazz Singer of Note

Tracey Wright, or someone like her, may perform in your school or your community. It's all courtesy of the U.S. military services. Part of Tracey's job is to talk to young, aspiring musicians about joining the military and to explain how to have a music career in the armed services. The other part of her job is singing.

Master Sergeant Tracey is the lead vocalist for The Airmen of Note, the jazz ensemble of the premier U.S. Air Force Band, based at Bolling Air Force Base, in Washington, DC. She spends a great deal of her time rehearsing and performing.

"Each year we go out on two 2-week tours and perform eight jazz heritage concerts. During the school year we

U.S. AIR FORCE BANDS: In the U. S. Air Force regional bands, entry level is Airman, approximately $17,000 per year. (if have college credits, may come in as Airman First Class, slightly higher pay)
In the U. S. Air Force National Band, come in as Tech Sergeant, $30,000 per year.

# TRACEY'S CAREER PATH

Sings in church choirs, attends college

Joins Air Force, medical transcriptionist

Enters talent show, tours with Tops in Blue

average 50 to70 college clinics. We support 120 to 150 military functions. Sometimes the big band plays; sometimes it is just me and a rhythm section (drummer, bass, and piano) if the gathering is small, like a dinner party for foreign dignitaries."

In the three years Tracey has been in Washington, she has performed at the White House several times. "Normally during the Christmas season, the band is there 10 to 12 nights from December 1st. It is lots of fun. President Clinton sat in with us one year, playing his saxophone. That was a hoot. He makes it a point to come up and shake everyone's hand."

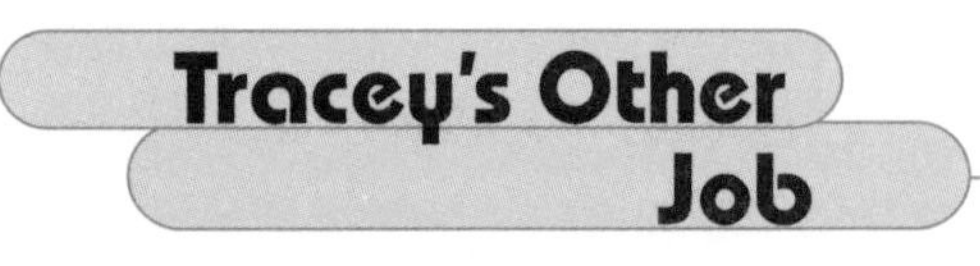


Tracey's other job is Superintendent of Equal Opportunity Outreach. She represents her whole squadron in her educational and recruitment efforts at schools, colleges, and other institutions that have a large minority population. "It's fun meeting the people and the students and telling them about

Joins regional band, sings R&B, Country and Broadway songs

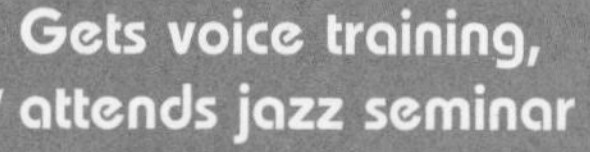

Gets voice training, attends jazz seminar

Joins Big Band at Robins AFB, sings jazz

the Air Force Bands. The Concert Band and the Airmen of Note Jazz Ensemble are the two largest groups. Then there are The Singing Sergeants (chorus), The Strolling Strings (orchestra), The Ceremonial Brass (marching), High Flight (popular music), and Silver Wings (country music). From the Concert Band we also have woodwind quartets and quintets, as well as chamber music ensembles."

Many people think of a marching band or a concert band when they think of the military. Tracey's job is to let students know that the career opportunities are quite broad. As new recruits, musicians go through six weeks of basic training, including some time playing in the drum and bugle corps.

"My job is part of a new program. It may turn into a career job in the Air Force. I have to do a lot of paperwork and computer work and keep a detailed record of everything I do, to help make a decision about the value of this work." Tracey gets to do a lot of her paperwork and planning in her office at home. "A lot of people are doing that now. Some of our music arrangers do 90 percent of their work at home because there are fewer interruptions."

## Rehearsals and Performances

To attend rehearsals, Tracey drives to the base from her home in Stafford, Virginia, where she lives with her husband, Derrick, and her 7-year-old son, Tyler. She arrives around 9:00 a.m. and rehearsals usually last about four hours. Today, the Airmen of Note are going over, phrase by

Joins Airmen of Note as lead vocalist

Promoted to Master Sergeant, in charge of Equal Opportunity Outreach

phrase, the numbers they will record on their new CD of contemporary jazz. When the group has a performance or is on tour, rehearsal schedules vary, depending upon when and where they are performing.

"Jazz has become a passion of mine. The music is so free; you can move around vocally, you are not constricted. I'm inclined to want to imitate the band instruments, the horns, woodwinds, anything I can make my voice sound like. I like to scat—using my vocal chords in ways I never thought imaginable."

Tracey's favorite singer role models are Sarah Vaughn and Ella Fitzgerald. "I listen to the way they sing and try to get into their heads. I recently discovered Keely Smith, which opened another avenue. I never get bored. I can sing one song hundreds of different ways."

Tracey's calls her relationship with the band wonderful. "I'm the baby sister of the group. I'm not afraid to take chances. If I hear them play a certain line in the solo of a song, I'll ask them to teach it to me. The guys are great to me, but there are two people who I worry to death musically—our musical director, Senior Master Sergeant Joe Eckert, and Senior Master Sergeant Saul Miller. Then when I get on stage to perform and actually do that bit and give them a look, it makes them feel good about it."

The band is preparing for an overseas tour of their Glenn Miller program. (Glenn Miller was a famous band leader who served in World War II. His musical style and arrangements—the Glenn Miller sound—are still played today.) "We

## CAREER CHECKLIST

### You'll like this job if you ...

- Are musical, have a good ear
- Are flexible, will sing all kinds of music
- Have an easy-going attitude
- Like to perform for small and large groups
- Will work hard, practice, and keep learning
- Will work long, irregular hours
- Like to travel

## How the U.S. Air Force Organizes Its Musicians

The Air Force has two premier bands—The U.S. Air Force Band in Washington, DC, and the U.S. Air Force Band of the Rockies in Colorado Springs, CO—and ten regional bands. Bands are organized so that they may be subdivided into several smaller musical units, which often have their own group names. All performing units will play for military functions and community relations functions. Examples of performing units include:

**Concert Band**: Performs concert, patriotic, and popular entertainment music at high school, college, university, and civic concerts.

**Marching or Ceremonial Band:** Performs military marching and patriotic music at civic and military ceremonies or parades.

**Jazz/Show Band:** Performs traditional "big band" and contemporary music.

**Popular Music Ensemble:** Performs a variety of popular music to include rock, Top 40, country, and "oldies."

**Chamber Ensemble:** Performs a variety of music using different instrumentation in concert settings.

**Protocol Combo:** Performs background, dinner and dance music for official military social functions.

**Individual Musicians:** Buglers for funerals, solo vocalists, pianists, or other instrumentalists may perform for official functions or ceremonies.

will be spending about 15 days in Europe recreating the Glenn Miller music. We'll have a group of Singing Sergeants, the strings, the concert band, and jazz. It is a big production; we'll perform on military bases and in some civilian venues." The band members will dress in the WWII style pink and green uniforms, but Tracey will wear a gown.

"The best part is when people come up after the show and tell me what they were doing when the song was first released, who they were dating, how it felt. Seeing them light up going down memory lane is one of the biggest thrills for me."

For most military performances, band members wear mess dress. For Tracey, that means she will wear a long blue skirt, short jacket, and white tuxedo shirt. When Airmen of Note do the community gigs, they wear regular blue duty uniforms that have a silver stripe down the pants' leg and a jacket with ribbons. Tracey can choose to wear either slacks or a skirt, since she's the only woman in the group.

## Discovered in the Air Force

Tracey grew up in Alexandria, Virginia. While she sang in church choirs, and she, her sisters, and cousins performed in talent shows, she didn't think of singing as a career. In a high school career-testing program, she found that one of the jobs she would be good at was hospital work. After she graduated in 1981, she decided to join the Air Force and work in a hospital, but she had to wait to get in. She took college courses, and was able to join in 1986. Because of those credits she came in as an Airman First Class.

At that time, Tracey didn't even know a musical career was a possibility. She became a medical file clerk and moved up to medical transcriptionist at Robins Air Force Base in Warren Robins, Georgia. But one Christmas dance, the deejay was playing The Christmas Song (Chestnuts Roasting on an Open Fire), and the record kept skipping, which made Tracey mad. Her date jokingly said "Go up there and sing it" and she did. A member of the band heard her and suggested she audition for the regional band stationed at Robins. She

**Jazz is a hard field to get into. I know I wouldn't be able to work and grow as a vocalist and have a steady paycheck like I do here if I weren't in the military.**

didn't think she'd have a chance because she didn't have the required college degree in music, so she said no. Later, she entered and won several talent shows and was selected to tour with an organization called Tops in Blue. She joined the group of 30 people who traveled all over the world for one year, putting on a musical show for the servicemen.

"I was really lucky to have the opportunity to perform with Tops In Blue, since I had never performed before. Tops In Blue taught me how to perform, which gave me a head start in performing with the USAF Band."

When Tracey returned to Robins AFB to perform, people from the regional band saw her, and at the end of the tour, they offered her an audition. This time she took it. "They hired me that day. I found out later that it took special waivers to get me hired because I didn't have a degree in music."

Now in the band career field, Tracey discovered that the Air Force would provide professional training. She received vocal instruction from Mrs. Johnnie Davis of Atlanta, and learned to breathe properly and control her voice. She went to a professor to learn to sight read music. In 1994, she attended the Bud Shank Jazz Workshop, her introduction to jazz. "I've had a lot of good people giving me advice—about what musicians to listen to and study. I want to understand everything about a song, who wrote it, why they wrote it, and I listen to different vocalists who have recorded it."

## A Future in the Business

As a member of the band squadron, Tracey has learned not only the performance side but also the business side of music. The squadron is completely self-sufficient. Its members are responsible for doing everything from providing buglers for military funerals to putting on complex show productions like the Glenn Miller Show.

"I've learned so much about the business of music because it's part of our job. We find the gigs, do bookings, plan the logistics, figure the budget, do costumes, write scripts, have a production team and a technical team—audio and video people. If dancing is involved in a show, we hire a choreographer. From publicity to transportation, our unit handles everything. Because I work on recruiting new musicians, I get involved in auditions."

Tracey is preparing for the future. She's taking piano lessons and going to college to get a degree in music therapy. "I'll have a degree, and I'll be prepared to do local gigs, then go to New York." She hasn't decided when she will leave the Air Force, but she does plan to continue to perform.

# Jeanene Jarvie

Jeanene Jarvie

**Ballerina,** The Washington Ballet, Washington, DC

# Ballet Dancer

## From Plum Fairy to Romantic Heroine

Jeanene Jarvie has danced her way through 12 years as a member of two nationally known ballet companies. She's performed in Spain, Portugal, England, France, South Africa, and throughout the United States.

"An intriguingly odd ballerina with a tapering, supple torso and the prim but promising look of one of those movie heroines of old who is just about to take off her glasses," is the way a critic from *The New York Times* newspaper described her. The 27-year old ballerina, described by another critic as "tall and imperious," has been dancing since age 3. She has captured the attention of artistic directors and ballet audiences throughout the world. Currently, Jeanene dances with The Washington Ballet in Washington, DC.

Ballerina: The earnings of a member of a ballet company range from $375 per week to $1,000 per week and above.

# JEANENE'S CAREER PATH

- Dance and gymnastic lessons
- Ballet lessons at The Academy of The Dance
- Summer and apprenticeship with Boston Ballet II

Photo: Richard N. Greenhouse

Credit: Jeanene Jarvie & Peter Stark in "Double Contrasts"

Jeanene spends one and one-half hours a day in class (warm up) and then six hours in rehearsal. On days when there are no performances, she is at the studio by 10 in the morning and gone by 6. During performance days, she begins her work day at 10 or 11 and ends it about 12 hours later. In between class, rehearsal, and performances, there is time to put on make-up and costumes and to take breaks for lunch and dinner.

Jeanene loves spending her leisure time with her husband, their dog Boo, family, and friends. She also loves going to the beach, reading, writing, music, movies, sports, games, and shopping.

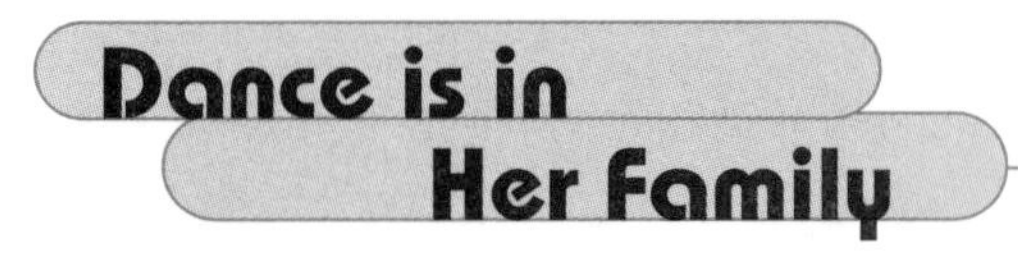

## Dance is in Her Family

Jeanene can't remember a time when she wasn't interested in dance. "Dance was a big part of my family. My mother and both her sisters danced, and my grandmother was a professional roller-skater." Jeanene's mother, a tap dancer, owns her own dance studio. One aunt danced on Broadway and another on cruise ships.

Joins The Boston Ballet

Gets own apartment, tours Spain

Joins The Washington Ballet, tours many countries

Jeanene's first classes were in her grandmother's basement, where her mother and aunts taught neighborhood kids. "My parents thought I would be a dancer because I danced all over the house from the time I was old enough to walk, practically."

After providing ballet, tap, jazz, modern dance, and gymnastics lessons for her daughter, it became evident to Jeanene's mother that Jeanene was best at ballet and liked it the most. The family lived in a small Pennsylvania town where there was no ballet dance studio of the caliber her mother desired. So, her mom drove Jeanene to Wilmington, Delaware, to the Academy of The Dance, for lessons from the time Jeanene was 10. Her mom, Jeanene, and her younger brother would leave directly after the kids got home from school. The studio was a full hour's drive from home and the lessons took two and one-half hours. Jeanene's mom and her little brother went shopping while Jeanene danced. "I was helped all the way along by my family, who spent four and one half hours every lesson day making sure I got my lessons. When I started taking formal lessons, I began to think maybe I could dance professionally."

"There were certainly sacrifices involved for everybody in my family as I prepared for this career, including me. I had two different sets of friends, school friends and ballet friends. The school friends would say, 'why can't you go to the football game or just come over and play?' But every day I had to get home from school to go to my ballet class. As I got older there were also rehearsals for performances. Friends would say, 'Can't you just skip the rehearsal?' They didn't really understand."

"I suppose what I liked best about it, and still do, is the fact that it is something you can never be perfect at. You always have to work to improve. I like the challenge and discipline of it. But I missed a lot of family events, especially later when I went away to dance."

## Summer School

When she was a teenager, her dance teachers encouraged Jeanene to apply for a summer ballet program out of town. Many young ballet dancers will explore a summer program connected with a professional dance company around ages 13 to 15. A summer program can expose young dancers to different teachers and styles of dance. Jeanene's teachers liked the program associated with The Boston Ballet, so Jeanene applied. But her parents told her she could only go if she got a scholarship. Soon, she received a letter telling her she had been accepted to the seven-week program and her tuition would be taken care of. Her mother knew it was a great opportunity, but her dad was a little less sure. Jeanene had just turned 15 and had never been away from home alone before, except to visit her aunt in New York City. Finally, her dad agreed to let her go, and that summer she took off for Boston.

"I cried for about two hours when I got there, but from then on I was fine, I loved it." Within the first week of her stay, the second Boston Ballet Company, BBII, asked her to stay permanently! The company of 16 young dancers was short a dancer and had to fill the position of apprentice ballerina. They were very interested in Jeanene's dance ability and also in her looks. The offer was a total surprise to Jeanene, her teachers, and her family. This company was the 'feeder' company for The Boston Ballet. It was a once-in-a-lifetime opportunity. When Jeanene's father came home from work the day the company had offered Jeanene the opportunity, he found her mom sitting on the porch crying. "Jeanene has been accepted into The Boston Ballet," she sobbed. Her mom knew this opportunity was too good to pass up. She was going to miss her daughter, who now would be dancing professionally and living away from home. Her dad wanted to know what Jeanene was going to do about school and where she was going to live.

## CAREER CHECKLIST

### You'll like this job if you ...

- Have the right body type
- Are flexible and have a certain ability for "turn out" (how your feet turn out and the way your hips are placed)
- Are very organized
- Are consumed by dance; will devote your life to dance and sacrifice other interests
- Can take hard criticism, will work to make things perfect
- Will move to any part of the world that has a program that accepts you

## The Youngest Apprentice

When her parents decided to let Jeanene join BBII, 15-year old Jeanene was the youngest apprentice the company had ever had. She lived with a family that had children in ballet lessons and took her school lessons from a school in Nebraska that offered a high school education by mail.

"I was living in a big city for the first time, taking the subway and buses by myself to get to class and rehearsal, and living away from home. It was really hard; I had to go to a job seven hours a day and then do homework at night. I couldn't have done it on my own, but fortunately, there was another girl, a senior, who was finishing her school that way. She took me under her wing, and we studied together. She's one of my best friends today. In fact, she was my maid of honor when I got married."

Photo: James E. Strickland

Jeanene apprenticed with BBII three years, touring all over New England. "I loved touring. We would go to other cities and stay in hotels. You got a 'per diem' to spend each day. I thought it was real freedom. We were pretty much a family. We were all thrown into that situation together and there was a real closeness there."

Jeanene's parents came to all the performances they could, even though it was a six-hour drive for them. They would leave on a Friday and return Sunday so that they could see Jeanene dance and spend a little time with her. During the holidays and the summers, when the company wasn't touring or performing in Boston, Jeanene got to go home. "Practically all my relatives live in that town, so my time was taken up with visiting with everybody."

She met her husband Sean in the dance company. "He is six years older. He had danced in Washington and New York. We were friends the first years and started dating later on. Many of the people in the company dated each other because those were the only people you saw, really."

Photo: James E. Strickland

## Big Changes at 18

When Jeanene turned 18, she was accepted into The Boston Ballet. "They didn't get rid of me in BBII, as they did with many of the apprentice dancers, so I thought I would get into the company. I felt more secure after I got in. It wasn't quite as stressful. I thought, okay, now I've made it in. Over the years I had seen people come and go. It's just a natural part of the ballet world."

It was also the year Jeanene got her first apartment, living with two of the other dancers. "This was a really big step. I had many discussions with my parents about whether or not it was the right thing to do." On their days off, the dancers would have to take care of their errands and their laundry, so there wasn't much time for socializing. But after a heavy performance schedule they were given a lay-off period. It was during this time that the dancers could really relax.

With The Boston Ballet, Jeanene usually performed as part of the corps dancers. The company put on all kinds of classical ballets. Every once in a while Jeanene would get a major part. A tour of Spain was one of the highlights of this period. "I was 19. We played beautiful theaters all over Spain. Some other dancers and I stayed over, because we had a lay-off period after our tour. We went to Italy and France on our own. We saw wonderful museums."

The Boston Ballet always performed The Nutcracker at home during the Christmas season. "We did about 50 performances of The Nutcracker in the month of December. Then we would get a week off in January. I always went home then."

While Jeanene loved The Boston Ballet, after she had been there a number of years, she began to want better parts. "They would bring in dancers from outside and give them these good parts. Sometimes I would get a part, but not often enough. I realized I would have to move to another company to

**I had tons of support and understanding from my family. We didn't have family dinners at 6:00 every night. We were on the road coming back from lessons.**

further my career. I was getting older, and I knew the dance career was short."

Jeanene took the train to Washington, DC, to visit Sean, who was dancing with The Washington Ballet by this time. She auditioned by taking a class, which the artistic director came to watch. The Washington Ballet made her an offer and she accepted. She went back to Boston to finish out the 1991-92 season and then moved to Washington. (Dancers sign a contract each year. The contract is offered in February or March and they have about four weeks to decide if they will sign. Once they sign, they are committed for the next season.)

By moving to Washington, Jeanene would be near Sean, closer to her family, and getting better parts because the company was smaller—20 dancers in contrast to the 60 that were in The Boston Ballet. Besides, the Washington company did more touring, which Jeanene loved, and also more contemporary works. She was ready for the change. "People think of me as a classical ballerina. That means everything is about line, placement, and technique. But I had done some contemporary works in Boston and wanted to do more. Being contemporary you have to have control of all those

Photo: James E. Strickland

things, but it's more about movement."

Her first season with Washington, the company toured Portugal. Jeanene began getting better parts right away. "I've had a lot of wonderful parts and worked with really good choreographers. I've gotten to dance more contemporary works. I also got to play the Sugar Plum Fairy in The Nutcracker, after playing virtually all the other parts. I've toured to London, France, South Africa, and Hawaii." Being in Washington also made it easier for Sean and Jeanene to get married, which they did in 1997. Sean, who was injured in an accident, is no longer dancing, but is still involved in the arts.

## First Time She's Hurt

Jeanene is recovering from her first serious injury in 12 years. "It's a sprain in the ligaments between my

Photo: James E. Strickland

hip and my back. I got hurt during a performance. It's really hard not dancing. I miss the exercise and the discipline. I miss the people at work."

She spends part of her day in aerobic exercise to keep fit while she isn't dancing (she can do aerobics but certain dance movements bother her), and thinking about what to do when she will no longer be able to dance. "I always thought I would have a baby or two later with Sean and then return to the company. The idea of being injured really didn't occur to me. I would like to teach after I finish dancing. I've taught a little bit over the past five years and I enjoy that. Some people go on to school to study for a different career, but I'd like to stay connected to dance and pass my knowledge and experience on to the dancers of tomorrow."

**Jeanene has danced in:**

**Classical Ballets**
Swan Lake
Giselle
Don Quixote
Sleeping Beauty
Romeo and Juliet
Cinderella
The Nutcracker

**Balanchine Ballets**
Agon,
Four Temperaments
Theme & Variations
Allegro Brillante
Who Cares?
Mozartinana
Scotch Symphony
Ballet Imperial

**Contemporary Works By**
Twyla Tharp
Mark Morris
BB Miller
Choo San•Goh
Graham Lustig
Nils Christe

# Nina Flyer

**Principal Cellist,** Women's Philharmonic, the Classic Philharmonic, and the Bear Valley Music Festival Orchestra; Instructor, University of the Pacific Conservatory of Music, San Francisco, CA.

Major in Music, Performance

# Cellist Recording Artist

## The Voice of the Cello

When Nina Flyer was in the first grade in the Chicago school system, she took violin lessons. Her mother and her two aunts had played the cello, but Nina wanted to be different. Already she loved classical music. Her favorite piece was Swan Lake, which she and her uncle Phil would listen to, and she would dance to. Fortunately for Nina and those who love her music, the family moved to a Chicago suburb the following year and Nina got to hear a cello player at a music demonstration for kids. "Despite the fact that I wanted to be different, I couldn't resist the cello. It is the instrument most like the human voice. It was the instru-

**Principal Cellist: Major Orchestra $70,000 – 90,000**
**Regional Orchestra $20,000 - $45,000**
**For film and commercial work residual checks**
**Recitals and chamber music concerts $100 to $1,500 and up, depending on experience and name**

ment that spoke to me, and I've never regretted the choice."

Today Nina is principal cellist with the Women's Philharmonic in San Francisco, the only professional women's orchestra in the United States. She also is the principal cellist at the Classic Philharmonic and, in the summer, the Bear Valley Music Festival. For two summers she has been on month-long tours to Japan in an orchestra that plays the music of Percy Faith and Henry Mancini. She records classical and film music, and plays on the CDs of popular musicians like Linda Rondstadt. She also is an instructor in cello and chamber music at the University of the Pacific Conservatory of Music. She and violinist James Stern (also at UOP) and his wife, pianist Audrey Andrist, recently formed a chamber music group called the Yerba Buena Ensemble, which is now the Chamber Ensemble in Residence with Noontime Concerts™ in San Francisco.

"For many years I had steady jobs with orchestras, but now I appreciate my freedom. I can pick and choose what I want to do. I can do a lot more solo work. If you want dependability in your life, this isn't the life, but if you want to have your own creative projects, then it is a good life."

## From CDs to the Women's Philharmonic

Nina's life is a potpourri of different creative activities. She is in the midst of arranging a tour and recording a CD of a new cello/piano version of the Carnival of Animals (arranged by her friend Mark Fish), with the actor

David Ogden Stiers as the narrator and Chie Nagatani as pianist. Mark Fish wrote the music to the children's book *Ferdinand The Bull*, and that along with the Carnival will make up a family concert that Chie, David, and Nina will perform.

On a recent CD by composer Lou Harrison, Nina played a suite with pianist Josephine Gandolfi and a suite with harpist Dan Levitan. "Dan Levitan approached me about this one. I had worked on another CD with him of Lou's music, and he said he had been approached by Peer Publishing to record The Suite for Cello and Harp and would I do it. I said sure, I would love to."

Later, Nina was asked to record the cello and piano suite on the same CD. She was playing concerts in Iceland at the time and didn't have as much time to prepare for the second piece. "When I got home, I practiced every spare minute I could find." The two pieces are quite different. The cello and harp piece was written in 1949 for some friends of the composer and the other in 1997. "Lou dedicated the second

movement of the 1997 piece to a friend who died of AIDS. It is highly emotional. The first and third movements are joyful and playful."

Nina is experienced at recording, having recorded in Jerusalem when she played principal cello with the Jerusalem Symphony; in Iceland when she played principal with the symphony and with her friend concertmistress Gudny Gudmundsdottir (G.G.) in a chamber group; and at other times throughout her career. "You must be 200 percent prepared for what's going to happen next when you are recording as a soloist. You have to know absolutely everything inside and out. Usually with classical music there is no budget for big mistakes; you have to do it right every time. It's a very different experience from performing live. You have to save your energy in recording. You can't give all of it all the time or you will be spent right away. And you have to have a path plotted for what you want to do and how you want to do it."

Nina says probably the most thrilling day of her life was recording a concerto by Shulamit Ran with the English Chamber Orchestra in London. The CD was nominated for two Grammys. "I grew friendly with Shulamit, an Israeli composer, through an odd set of circumstances. My mother had met a cellist in Chicago who knew Shulamit, and my mother got me in contact with her when I was in Israel. We became good friends. I was always trying to play her music. While I was working as the acting principal cellist with the San Diego Symphony, the Women's Philharmonic called me up and asked if I could get Shulamit to write a cello concerto. Shulamit was engaged in too many other activities at the time, but she said she had always thought a piece she had written originally for cello and piano would make a great cello and orchestra piece. She talked to her ex-husband, who is an arranger, and convinced him to arrange it.

"We performed it at the Women's Philharmonic and a friend who worked at KOCH records, Michael Fine, wanted to record it with the English Chamber Orchestra. Michael is an old friend from Jerusalem; I first met him when he interviewed me for the radio there. So that's how the whole project came about. We recorded it in this beautiful old church in London. We had one session to rehearse and record the piece. The orchestra was so fast. They picked it up right away, and they knew exactly what to do. We got it done with a few minutes to spare. I brought my dear friend, conductor JoAnn Falletta, and she conducted the orchestra. She had conducted the performance I did with the Women's Philharmonic, she knew

## CAREER CHECKLIST

### You'll like this job if you ...

- Are willing to roll up your sleeves and seek opportunities to perform
- Have a passion for your instrument, for classical music, and for performing
- Are fiercely independent
- Are creative
- Are very focused
- Are flexible

the piece, and for no fee she agreed to come. Without her I couldn't have done it in the little bit of time we had. In the entertainment industry, they can take lots more time with the recordings. For classical music you have to get it right in a much shorter amount of time."

"I was thrilled to be nominated for the Grammys. It was really my first solo. My friend G.G. and I had done something on a local Icelandic label years ago, but in terms of a big splash, this was my first."

Nina practices the cello every day. "The day I don't play the cello is a sad day." Sometimes she squeezes practice in between rehearsals with the Yerba Buena Ensemble and her teaching activities, sometimes between rehearsals at the Women's Philharmonic and solo recitals, sometimes after she gives a private lesson. While her preferred practice place is her home, it's not always possible to wait until she is home to practice, so she steals the time where she can. Occasionally she goes to Honolulu to play in the Honolulu Symphony, and of course, practicing at home is impossible then.

**You have to practice five, six, seven hours a day and learn the logistics of your instrument.**

## Playing for the Movies

Classical music concerts and recording sessions require an attitude of extreme seriousness, but Nina does other types of recording that require a different type of energy. "I feel more of a sense of freedom working on film music." She and many musicians from the San Francisco area go to Skywalker, film director George Lucas' San Raphael estate, where they record tracks for movies. "It's sort of a melting pot of musicians from the Bay area, freelancers, and symphony and opera people. Some musicians even come from Los Angeles. There are llamas and rolling hills and the place is gorgeous. We all have a great time up there. When you record, you are listening to something called a click track. You have earphones and you hear a beat, a tempo, and you play to that. It's pleasurable and fun, and it puts me in contact with the hot new composers in the movie industry, which is so different from the other things that I do. You go to the movies and hear what you've done. And it pays really well."

Nina has played with the Women's Philharmonic since 1988. "It's been a wonderful eye opener to see and appreciate the contribution women have made to music over the centuries. I'm so into it myself that when I have to play a recital, I try to include a woman's piece if I can. I love many of the orchestras I play with now and have played with in the past, but I really, really love the Women's Philharmonic. It has a sense of purpose. I feel like I am opening people's eyes to things they might not have heard before. We have had a huge impact all over the

United States. We've traveled all over and played at concerts where the conductors have had their curiosity whetted enough that they have gotten into women's music too. It's a sort of mission, but it's not that we don't have fun. We enjoy what we're doing and feel that we're doing something really good."

## All She Wanted to Do Was Play

Nina took private lessons in elementary and junior high school. In high school she studied cello with Frank Miller, the former principal cellist of the Chicago Symphony, and Carl Fruh. "These were very fine teachers. I was winning competitions and getting first place in 'All State.' I was so focused. All I wanted to do was to play."

For college, Nina got a scholarship to the Eastman School of Music in Rochester, New York. "Even though I am one dimensional in terms of career, I love literature and lots of other things outside music and there wasn't any of that at Eastman. I thought I would be able to take classes at the University of Rochester. But it was not really feasible because it was so intense, and there wasn't time to take the bus to the U of Rochester."

After two years at Eastman, Nina took off for Vienna, Austria. She studied there and then went to Paris for a year with her friend, clarinetist Torsten Rippe. "At this point my parents were asking if I would ever finish college. So I came back and enrolled in the University of Southern California in Los Angeles, where I had many relatives."

After graduation, Nina moved to New York and freelanced as a musician for a year. She then won the audition as a cellist for the New Jersey Symphony, where she stayed for two years. "It was my first orchestral job; I was just learning the ropes but it was a great first job. I lived in Manhattan and freelanced at the same time. I played with the Danish Ballet and played a tour with the Bolshoi Ballet."

## Iceland, Norway, and Israel

In New York, Icelandic violinist G.G., Nina's friend from Eastman, came to visit. She said there was an opening for a principal cellist in the Iceland Symphony and Nina got the job. She and G.G. played in a chamber music group that toured all over Europe. The conductor for the Iceland Symphony was also the conductor for the Bergen, Norway Symphony. He brought Nina to Bergen to be acting principal cellist while the principal went on sabbatical. "When they needed somebody in a certain place, I would go. It was a way to see the world. All my travels abroad helped me to know about human beings and different cultures. This is absolutely essential if you are to be a good musician."

When she felt it was time to move on from Iceland, Nina applied to be principal cellist in Jerusalem. She spent the summer in Italy performing with friends in a group called Solisti Aquilani and then went to audition in Jerusalem. Her friends had offered her a permanent position playing with the Italian group, but taking the position as principal cellist with the Jerusalem Symphony was the right career move, she says. She stayed in Jerusalem for six years, marrying Izzy, a mathematician who was crazy about classical music.

"It's important for musicians to play through concerts. I had a friend who would give these little soirées so that I could play as a sort of rehearsal before a recital, for example, at the Israeli museum. Izzy was at one of these where I played through some Brahms sonatas. I remember that I was delighted talking with him afterwards. He knew so much about music." The couple is now divorced, but Nina keeps in close contact with her stepdaughter, Noah, who has recently gone to Paris. "I'm re-living my Paris days through her."

# Sherri Edelen

Sherri Edelen

**Member** of Actor's Equity Union

Major in Theater

# Stage Actress, Singer

## Rehearsals Are the Best Part

Acting is really about finding yourself, says Sherri Edelen. Sherri, who is 37, keeps getting better roles every year. She attributes her staying power in the extremely difficult and competitive profession of stage acting to keeping a sense of balance in her life and coming from a place within herself that is truly honest.

"There are people who live and breathe theater and would do anything to get to Broadway. But I come from a background of looking at things realistically. Broadway actors don't really make a lot of money in comparison to the high cost of living in the New York City area. An actress friend who once lived there in her heyday told me, 'don't go unless you have a deep burn-

**Actor:** Salaries are usually low except for the best known performers. That is why actors take many different jobs that use their talents. They also do part-time work in nonrelated fields.
*Earnings for actors who are members of a union and sign a union contract:*
Broadway actors earn a minimum of $1,000 per week; Off Broadway actors earn from $380 to $650 per week. On tour, the actors earn an additional $100 a day.
Motion picture and television actors earn $500 to $1,750 for a 5-day week. Extras earn a minimum of $100 a day. According to individual contracts, actors get paid additional money (called residuals) when the TV show or film is rerun; film actors sometimes negotiate a percentage of the profits.

Source: *Career Information Center* (7th ed.). (1999). Macmillan

Listens to show tunes, goes to movies and theater

Graduates college

Works at Nashville Children's Theater

ing desire and you can't live without it. It will swallow you alive.'"

Sherri hasn't ruled out being on Broadway someday, but she does not have to have that to be happy as an actress. She recently bought a house in suburban Maryland, which is a symbol of her commitment to stay in the Washington, DC, area and find opportunities for acting. "I can still go on tour out of town to work, and I can go to New York in the spring, which is the audition season. But now I have a home base, which is important to me."

Credit: Steve Isom & Sherri Edelen "The Music Man" at Stages St. Louis

Sherri has worked steadily as an actress since arriving in Washington, DC, from her home town of Nashville in 1988. She started in a cabaret atmosphere, did ensemble work in a non-union tour, and came back to the area to do better roles in well-known productions. Now she is broadening her possibilities by marketing herself for industrial and training films, print advertisements, and other less glamorous but highly lucrative jobs. Sherri has worked six jobs doing on-camera work in the

three-month period since she started looking for this type of work to tide her over between shows. "I've done a sexual harassment training film, print ads for hospitals, and some related types of work."

Sherri also works part-time for a talking books program through the U. S. Library of Congress. "The blind and physically challenged are the only people who can check out these particular books. It's a good service, and it makes me feel good to do it. I'm a reviewer and I check for errors on the tape. The company is slowly working me into doing narration. It's not easy because you have to understand all the characters in the book and have different voices for each one. This is something I can do to keep the money coming in. I also learn a new side of the business.

"I used to apply for unemployment benefits, but now that I have this side job, I don't need to. Often there is a sense of shame about taking unemployment, but not for actors."

Sherri also is working on an idea to take theater into the schools. By introducing historic figures who have overcome their personal obstacles to obtain their dreams, she hopes to teach kids self-respect. She loves performing for children. "They are so honest in their reactions."

## She Comes East

When she first came to the East coast, Sherri was not a union actor. She never had trouble finding work. She came with a group of young actors to the FishMarket in Baltimore, a nightclub where there they performed in a cabaret-type atmosphere. Then Sherri landed a chorus role in the non-union tour of *Me and My Gal*. "It was my first bus and truck tour. It went all over the United States and into Canada, with stops in several cities—Seattle, Kansas City, and Ft. Lauderdale, among others.

"There were a lot of one, two, and three nighters, and you spent a lot of time on the bus. It was a 27-week tour. After the tour the company was going to do the show at Harrah's Casino in Atlantic City, and I could have stayed with it, but by that time I thought eight months was about enough for me. I was ready to do something new. I had heard Toby's Dinner Theater in Maryland was doing *Sunday in the Park with George*. Toby came to see me on our last stop of the tour in Philadelphia. I auditioned for them in the hotel room. I got the part of Dot, and got to wear some great, original costumes. (The musical is about the life of painter George Seurat and Dot is his fictitious lover.) That led to my staying in the Baltimore/Washington area."

## A Team Player

One reason Sherri works so much is that she is extremely talented. She can act and sing, and although not a dancer, she can move well. Another reason Sherri finds work is that she is a team player. "You have to do what is best for the show. You may not always agree with a director's concept, but you are hired to bring that concept to life."

Sherri's latest performance (in St. Louis, Missouri) is a seven-week contract at Stages St. Louis. She plays the lead female role, Marian the librarian, in *The Music Man*. "I usually play the second banana and not the ingénue or leading lady. I'm known as a belter (I sing out Ethel Merman style), and Marian is a soprano role. Although I can sing soprano, it's my first leading role in that style, and I enjoyed the challenge."

Sherri has worked Stages St. Louis before. The director, Michael Hamilton, invited her to audition for one of the daughters in *Fiddler on The Roof*. "I asked him if I could sing for Marian and he seemed unsure. I don't think he had ever heard me sing soprano and I wanted him to know another aspect of my voice. I thought I could get a chorus role in the show. After I auditioned for the Fiddler part, a slightly soprano role, Michael asked if I could sing a little of the Marian role. But I hadn't prepared anything. He had me learn a little of the music on the spot, and I got a callback. (A callback is a second audition. Actually, you can go

## CAREER CHECKLIST

### You'll like this job if you ...

- Love to perform in front of others
- Are a team player; can take direction well
- Will listen to criticism and improve
- Can take rejection and won't get discouraged
- Are willing to do many different things to earn a living
- Love story telling and making up stories
- Don't mind being away from home a lot

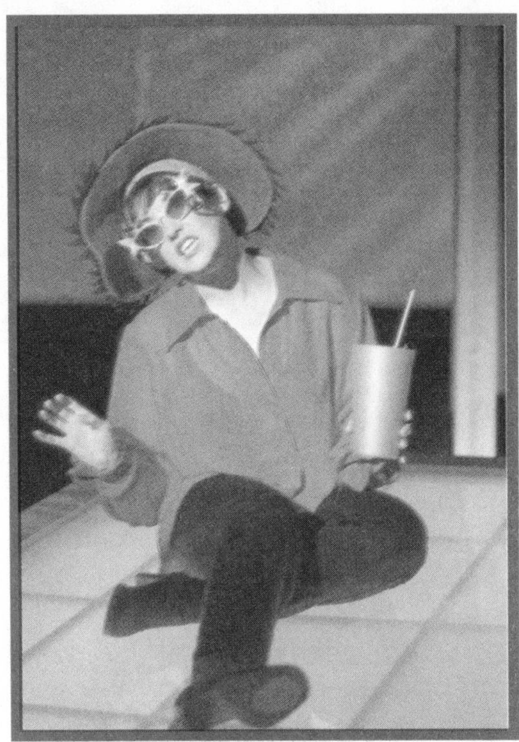

Credit: "Tell Me On a Sunday" at Signature Theater

to many callbacks until the director decides which actor he wants to do the role.) A month later, Stages St. Louis offered me the part. I was quite surprised."

When the role calls for it, Sherri gets coaching from people with expertise in song and dance. Recently she worked with musical director George Fulgini-Shakar. He helped her prepare for a role as the star and only actor of *Tell Me On a Sunday* at Signature Theater in Alexandria, Virginia, and for Marian the librarian. "I still take classes when I have the time and hope to study at the Shakespeare Theater in DC someday."

## Long Days

At Stages St. Louis, Sherri will perform in nine shows a week. On Saturdays, one show starts at 5:00 p.m. and the other at 9:00 p.m.. "I wondered how could I possibly do two shows back to back, but they provided a meal for the cast in between, and it became my favorite performance day of the week. The hard part was getting up on Sunday for a 2:00 p.m. show."

Because Sherri is an Equity actor, Stages St. Louis has to provide housing. Being an Equity actor also has other advantages. "The pay is greater than nonequity actors make. You have health insurance as long as you work a certain number of weeks a year, and there are rules to protect you from overlong rehearsal hours." The Equity actors pay a hefty initiation fee to join the union plus work dues, which all are deducted from the paycheck.

"I got my Equity card when I was an understudy at the Kennedy Center in Washington for a show called *Pump Boys and Dinettes*. I understudied for the two female roles in the show. The actress who played Rhetta had her wisdom teeth taken out, then got an infection, so I had the role for nearly two weeks."

Before *Pump Boys and Dinettes*, Sherri got involved with Signature Theater in their production of *Assassins*. "I received the Helen Hayes Award nomination for my performance in that show. Once I got my Equity card, I didn't think I'd ever work for them again. But as Signature grew rapidly, they began hiring union actors, and I went back in 1996 to do *The Rink*, for which I received another Helen Hayes nomination. The next spring I did *Sunday In The Park with George*, which was a collaboration between Arena Stage and Signature. The director of *Sunday in the Park* and the artistic director at Signature, Eric D. Schaeffer, were taking the musical *big* on the road for national tour, and I was lucky to be cast in the ensemble and have the role of Diane."

**It seems like I'm always making opportunities for myself by asking or writing directors about playing certain parts that they don't typically see me doing.**

## A Solo Performance

One of Sherri's best roles was *Tell Me On a Sunday*, which is half of an Andrew Lloyd Weber work titled *Song & Dance*. *Tell Me On a Sunday* is for a solo artist who has to act, sing, and move. "I saw it on Broadway with Bernadette Peters, and I loved it. Later I started thinking it was something I could do. When I was looking for work about five years ago, I wrote a letter to Eric Schaeffer at Signature and suggested it. That was a bold move! I don't know if he remembered this or not, but when he was looking for a show to complement the rest of his season, he asked me if I wanted to do it."

Sherri says it was scary being out on stage by herself for the entire hour and one half of the production. "If anything went wrong, I was the only one who could get myself out of a problem. I gained immense amounts of confidence as I learned to rely on myself."

## A Middle America Gal

Sherri grew up in what she calls "a typical American family." "My dad came home every night at a regular time, and my mom stayed home and took care of us. There were always lots of kids in the neighborhood. My dad loved movies and theater and MGM musicals. I grew up going to the movies and listening to big bands and show tunes. In high school I got parts in the school plays, but I decided to major in English at college and teach. Acting at that time didn't seem like a very realistic career.

"However, I studied dance at my college, Middle Tennessee State University, and they put on concerts in the theater department. I began hanging out more and more in the theater department and eventually I was hooked. When I told my dad I was interested in being an actor he said, 'I hope you're prepared to starve.' He knew it was a difficult life. He had grown up in the depression and valued stability and security. As it turns out, my parents have supported me every step of the way."

"The last three years in the theater department I excelled, whereas in English, I wasn't that good. I hated comparative writing, although I loved reading and story telling. Since theater is a heightened form of storytelling, I ended up graduating with a theater major."

Credit: "Tell Me On a Sunday" at Signature Theater

After graduation, Sherri worked for TicketMaster, selling tickets to concerts and plays, and did community theater on the side. She took some nine-to-five jobs and pursued her theater interests but didn't get paid for acting. Eventually she got hired for the Nashville Children's Theater, where she did get paid for acting. She performed such classics as *The Diary of Anne Frank* and *The Lion, the Witch, and the Wardrobe*. Then she got a job in Opryland, an amusement park and hotel in Nashville. From there she found work at the FishMarket in Baltimore, and her career was launched.

# Beth Wood

Beth Wood

**Singer / Songwriter,** Pop and Folk, Atlanta, GA

Major in English literature

# Singer Songwriter

## Music is Her Way to Connect

Beth Wood's music is a mixture of ballads and break-up songs—a blend of rock, pop, jazz, blues, and folk. But even though she is influenced by a number of musical traditions, she has a unique sound. Beth is a singer / songwriter of unusual talent. She writes and performs from the heart. Listening to her is like riding a train through the mountains with breathtaking views on an autumn day—you would like to stay on and enjoy those subtle fall colors forever.

Making it in the music business is never easy. Beth's story illustrates how hard it can be, even for someone with so much talent. Tenacity and love of performing have helped her to develop staying power. Her favorite thing is connecting with audiences. "I

**Singer / Songwriter: Pop and Folk: Performances at colleges and universities pay up to $1,000 per show. After expenses a performer can make $400 to $500 a night. Other venues pay much less but have tip jars. Income from records can vary, depending on the amount of play your records get and how many you sell.**

don't want to be on the cover of *Rolling Stone*," she says. "I just want to keep making music."

With three CDs now to her credit, Beth will be heard by more people each year. Currently she tours colleges throughout the United States; plays in restaurants, coffee houses, and other venues; opens for well-known national performers; and gets play on the radio. She recently moved from the Asheville, North Carolina, area to Atlanta, Georgia, where she recorded her latest CD, *Late Night Radio*. One critic wrote:

"The songs shimmer with a vibrancy, enthusiasm, and warm passion that frames Wood's powerfully expressive voice. Whether she's singing about the travels of her stolen Miles Davis album in the fittingly named 'My Miles Davis Kind of Blue,' or articulating her love of 'Late Night Radio' as she drives across the country in the jangly title track, Wood crafts her songs with intricate touches and a cogent eye for life's joys and frustrations."

Beth's other CDs—*New Blood*, recorded in 1998, and *Wood Work*, recorded two years earlier—have that same originality, although *Late Night Radio* is the most polished of the three. The combination of a classically trained voice, a fine instrumentalist, and an original songwriter makes for good listening.

## She Played Piano From Age Five

Beth grew up in Lubbock, Texas, in a family where there was always music in the house. Her mother played the piano. Her father simply loved music. Beth herself was musical from an early age, with piano lessons at five, and violin and harp lessons throughout high school. She liked to listen to pop and rock, turning the radio dial until she found the female singers and songwriters.

"I went to camp around age 10, and we did a skit from *Annie*, the musical. It was the first time I knew I could sing." The next year, she attended a music camp at Brevard College in Brevard, North Carolina.

In high school she sang in the choir—both traditional choral music and show tunes—and played in the orchestra.. She was Minnie the hatmaker in a production of *Hello Dolly*. "I had hopes of being a piano player when I was younger, but as I got older my hands didn't get any bigger, and I realized that wasn't the direction I was going to take." High school also was a time to soak up poetry and other literature. "Being exposed to other people's way with words has given me a good foundation for songwriting."

## Studies Music and English Literature

Remembering teachers from the music camp at Brevard fondly, Beth applied for college there. She stayed two years, studying voice. But something about the intensely competitive nature of classical voice training took the fun out of it, and Beth left the school to enroll at the University of Texas at Austin, where she changed her major to English literature. She sang in the college choir and played piano in the college's rehearsal rooms.

Beth missed not having music in her life on a daily basis. It was sometimes difficult to get the rehearsal rooms to play the piano. One day she bought a used guitar with money she had saved from a summer job, and she started teaching herself chords and some simple songs. As soon as she felt comfortable on the guitar, she answered an ad on the choir bulletin board for a backup singer. She got the job.

The band was called Raspberry Jam. She played rhythm guitar and percussion and sang backup. "That was great fun for me, different from the classical stuff I had done. With no structure, there was so much room for creativity. I always liked harmonizing. We did mostly folky, three-part harmony stuff and played in coffee houses and bars in Austin."

## The Makings of a Songwriter

Beth had fiddled with songwriting in high school, but she never dreamed that she would be a songwriter. Now, in a band where she could showcase some of her work, she took songwriting seriously. She would come up with an idea and then try it out on the band. Often they would give her suggestions. The band started working some of the songs into their act, and after about a year, Beth had five of her own songs in Raspberry Jam's repertoire. "They were definitely autobiographical—lots of good breakup songs."

Beth briefly considered teaching English while in college, but she was not too concerned about finding a way to make a living. She just enjoyed learning during the day and playing music at night. However, when she graduated from college, she felt compelled to make a decision about what to do with the rest of her life. She knew she wanted to play music. The question was how to do that and make enough money to live. She and the drummer from the band formed a duo and continued to play in coffee shops around Austin for tips. During the day, she worked at a real estate developer's office, first as a receptionist and then doing administrative work. "The people there were supportive of my

## CAREER CHECKLIST

### You'll like this job if you ...

- Are comfortable being on display for other people
- Have the discipline to practice every day
- Will persevere through any discouragement
- Like the idea of connecting with others through music
- Are creative and love both words and music

music. They would come and see me play. Austin is a hard town to make a living as a musician. There are so many musicians that you have to play for free sometimes just to get heard."

Beth applied to a music school in Boston—Berkley College of Music. When she got accepted, she was forced to decide if she really wanted to start all over again studying music (the college didn't have a masters program so she would have to begin with a bachelors again) or try to make it in the music business without any more formal training. She decided to make a record instead of going back to school. That way, when she played, she would have something to give to her audiences to remember her by.

She moved home to live with her parents, who had moved to Dallas, and got an office job. She borrowed $6,000 from her grandmother. On the weekends she would drive to Austin, where she bought time at a recording studio. "I found the studio through some friends who had recorded there. It was reasonably priced and it was convenient to my musician friends, so I could have them play on the record. It can get really expensive when you are paying for the recording time yourself. It's sort of like sitting in a taxicab and watching the meter go up. This studio was $35 an hour, which was reasonable then and is really cheap these days. We probably took five or six weekends, doing it piecemeal, so that everyone could play together. It was hard driving back and forth to Austin, but I wanted to get my songs out there." *Wood Work* contains

**Performing is a huge part of my life.**

the 11 songs Beth had written to that point. "I didn't have a grand plan for what to do with the CD when it was finished. I just wanted to have CDs at shows and sell them there."

About the time the CD came out, Beth got to know the members of a well-known Southeastern U.S. band, Jupiter Coyote. The band played Austin one night and some friends of Beth introduced her to its members. "We got to talking about music and played some music for each other, and they really liked what I was doing. They had just started an independent record label for their own music, and they approached me about recording on their label. Naturally I was thrilled. It was a strange connection. They had gone to Brevard and so had I, but we hadn't known each other. Their label, Autonomous Records, licensed *Wood Work*, which means they had the right to distribute it, and that's how it got into the record stores."

Beth continued to play Austin and got gigs in Dallas by sending out her

> Music is a vehicle to connect to other people. It's rewarding to make that connection with other people and have them say, yes, I've felt like that before.

CD and then auditioning. Jupiter Coyote asked her to open shows for them when they were in town, a big boost for her career. After wearing out the pavement between Austin and Dallas with engagements in both places, she finally moved back to Austin and started working for the Austin real estate developer again. "I didn't need to live at home anymore, now that the record was out."

## A Full-time Musician

Beth realized it would be too hard to make a living, solely as a musician, in Austin. "Texas is a difficult place to tour from because it is so spread out and there are only a few cities you can play. I was watching what Jupiter Coyote was doing and it seemed to me like touring the Southeast was a smart thing to do. Everything is closer together and there are more cities to play."

When John from Jupiter Coyote, who had a big house in Brevard, offered Beth a room to stay in, Beth moved to Brevard. She started playing in Asheville, other parts of North Carolina, South Carolina, and finally Tennessee. Venues typically would pay her about $75 a night for her first appearances and put out a tip jar. She was able to make enough to pay her bills that way. "I wasn't saving any money, but I wasn't going into debt either. It felt really good. It was nice not having a day job, and I was doing something I really wanted to do."

A year after she got to Brevard, Autonomous Records struck a deal with a major record label and signed Beth for a new CD. *New Blood* was financed by Autonomous. It was recorded in Atlanta and co-produced by Kristian Bush and Don McCollister. Beth had met Bush, who was a musician and produced records, while on a performing tour. McCollister was the owner of the studio where *New Blood* was recorded. "I made the decision about what songs to include," Beth says. "The producers helped decide what instruments would go on what songs. They generally helped me to package the music better. For example, if I had a song that was 6 and 1/2 minutes long, they might say, this is a little too long. Let's cut this verse. They helped me to fit the songs into a format that would be valuable commercially. They also brought in other musicians—people who were really wonderful to work with. It was something I definitely couldn't have accomplished on my own. It was what I really needed at the time. I had the musical know-how, but I didn't have the technical know-how."

*New Blood* was well-received. It started getting good play on the radio. It was distributed all over the United States. It eventually charted in the

**I've learned a lot about the business side of the music business.**

top 20 of the national AAA radio charts, the adult alternative to the top 40. "It was really cool to see all these people in places I had never even been buying my records." But three months after the release of *New Blood*, Autonomous Records lost its funding and the business shut down. Since Autonomous had financed the record, they owned it, but they weren't distributing it because they didn't exist anymore. Finally, after lengthy negotiations, Beth was able to buy *New Blood* back from Autonomous by borrowing money from her dad.

Jupiter Coyote's management company had a manager who liked Beth's work and stayed with her when Autonomous folded. Her manager is responsible for booking her in venues around the area and getting her publicity. He's working now to get *Late Night Radio* played throughout the country. Just as with *New Blood*, it will be available at the listening post at Borders Books and Music, and her manager expects it to top the AAA charts like *New Blood* did.

**You need a certain level of knowledge just to protect yourself and make sure good things are happening for your music.**

Through a musician friend, Beth met an agent who books acts at colleges. The agent got her into the college market. Beth will drive to a city, usually alone although sometimes if it is close she will take a band, and play a college. "I always play barefoot. I started doing that back in Austin and it just feels right." Then she'll spend the night and drive the next morning to another city and another college. By the end of 1999, she had played more than 150 shows in 28 states. "It pays much better than other venues and through this I was able to save up enough money to record the third album, *Late Night Radio*. I like the college kids, the exposure, and connecting with new audiences." Typically she will play five or six shows a week.

*Late Night Radio* was recorded in Atlanta, where Beth has recently established her home. "It's a good town to meet musicians. It's very important to keep in touch with the musicians you've met and to keep meeting new ones. Musicians have taught me so much, not just about music, but about the business side of it. You have to have good timing and good connections in this business."

## GROUNDBREAKERS

### Kentucky Singer and Balladeer

One of the most popular interpreters of the traditional ballads of Kentucky, Jean Ritchie (1922-) was the youngest of 14 children in a family that sang for entertainment. Before she started her singing career, she was a teacher, a supervisor of elementary schools, and a social worker. In 1948, she sang publicly at a folk music festival at Columbia University. The next year she devoted herself full time to her music. She appeared regularly on a local radio program, performed at Royal Albert Hall in Britain and for the BBC radio, and documented the music of Appalachia in several books.

Source: Women's History Project

# Terry Lyn Berliner

Terry Lyn Berliner

**Director and Dance Choreographer,** Brooklyn, NY

Major in English and Creative Writing; Master's in Dance Choreography, University of California at Los Angeles

# Choreographer

## A Passion for Dance and Storytelling

Terry Lyn Berliner often spends a good part of her day working with dancers to teach dance steps. A typical theater day is 10 to 6 with a break for lunch. Before the rehearsal period begins, Terry will have prepared by fully understanding the script and score and having the numbers she wants to choreograph mapped out in her head. She also will have worked with the musical director and the show's director to understand the production values.

"I may think a number should be choreographed in a certain way. I work with the director so that the movement conveys the right message."

Terry often blocks out a schedule during the week before rehearsals so that she can be the most efficient dur-

Choreographer: "Year one or ten you make nothing doing what you love or you get paid between nothing and $10,000 a year. Then you get more paying jobs, work in theater, and you make $25,000 a year, that's pretty darn good." Terry Lyn Berliner

ing the rehearsal period, normally about four weeks. "You are working toward the deadline of opening night, so you have to have an agenda of how to get there." She teaches dancers in blocks of one and one-half hours, working with the show's director, who has the responsibility for the overall vision of the production.

"You can't teach the dance unless you have the movement in your own body, so I have to know how to demonstrate all the steps." Terry will refer to notes she made during her preparation time to help her remember what she had in mind for each number. She will have practiced the movements in her home or in a studio to prepare for rehearsal.

"Even though I do a lot of work before I walk into the room with the actors or dancers, sometimes the dance works, but sometimes it needs modifications to make it work. You sketch it out with the dancers and then go back and figure out what didn't work. You are always refining the dance numbers. Later, you may see from the audience reaction that they aren't responding the way you

Graduates college, studies dance in London

Studies acting at American Conservatory Theatre

Masters in dance choreography from UCLA

wanted, so you continue to refine the dance. But you teach the basic movements early in the rehearsal period so you can work on perfecting as you get closer to opening night."

## She Always Loved Storytelling

It was the passion to tell stories that propelled Terry into a career as dance choreographer and stage director. Terry studied English and creative writing in college, and she found that she could combine her dance background with her love of storytelling to create stories in dance. She has been making a living in New York for six years, working as assistant director on and off Broadway, and as a choreographer, director, and assistant director in regional theater and summer stock. She also choreographs fashion shows, benefits, and awards events, and works as an associate editor on a stage directors' and choreographers' professional journal.

"It was probably at least six months before I could earn any money in the theater after coming to New York. You have to be willing to work for free to get your foot in the door," Terry says. "Today my life is a roller coaster. I have to be constantly finding new sources of work. I do two or three jobs at a time to make it, which is actually kind of interesting. I never get bored because there is so much variety. I'm just getting ready to direct *Guys and Dolls* in regional theater in upstate New York, but I'm also directing a show for a downtown festival next month, and I'm choreographing a fashion show next month

at the same time. I'll assistant direct on Broadway and be paid a lot of money. Then I'll go off and direct or choreograph a show for very little money. My life is a montage."

When I work with young people, I tell them you have to be willing to work for free and you will get a job out of it eventually if you do excellent work.

## A Natural Dancer

Born of a mother who "did the twist when she was pregnant," Terry took to dance immediately. She grew up in Los Gatos, California, where she took dance lessons from ages 3 through 16, mostly dancing jazz and tap. She even talked her teacher Sally Fraizer into letting her take dance classes to satisfy P.E. requirements in high school. The summer after her junior year, her dad arranged for Terry to attend the month-long American Dance Festival at Duke University in North Carolina.

"It was an eye-opener, coming from a tiny studio where all we did was jazz and tap, to have these exceptional teachers and students. I was one of the youngest people there. I took modern dance with Diane Gray and that changed my life. At the time, she was a Martha Graham dancer. She became my mentor. It was my first experience with modern dance, and I said, this is me. I wanted to be like Diane. She was so stoic and beautiful and strong, and she seemed so clear and expressive.

"Diane said, 'You should come to New York and go to the Martha Graham school.' I knew as soon as she said it, that was what I needed to do. When I got home, I told my dad and he said, 'Great, I'll help you do that.' He was the type of person who believed people should do the work they love. After I graduated from high school, my dad helped me find an apartment in New York. It was a nice building with a doorman, which everybody thought was the right thing for a young girl to do. The dance classes were only a few blocks away. I

## CAREER CHECKLIST

### You'll like this job if you ...

- Love to dance
- Like to tell stories
- Enjoy teaching people
- Have a good visual sense
- Have lots of family support
- Won't need a steady paycheck, can live with uncertainty
- Are willing to pay your dues

## GROUNDBREAKERS

**Choreographer/Anthropologist**

Katherine Dunham (1910-) danced and choreographed on stages throughout the world during the 1940s and 1950s. She specialized in Caribbean, African, and African-American dance movements. She studied modern dance and ballet in Chicago and joined with a member of the Chicago Civic Opera Company to establish an African-American dance group and later the Chicago Negro School of Ballet. She studied anthropology at the University of Chicago and then studied Caribbean African-based ritual dance. Dunham received a Guggenheim fellowship in 1937 to study dance in Haiti, Jamaica, Martinique, and Trinidad. Besides choreographing dances from the movements of these cultures, she presented lectures at Yale, University of Chicago, the Royal Anthropological Society of London, and the Anthropological Societies of Paris and Rio de Janeiro.

In 1943 the Katherine Dunham School of Arts and Research opened in New York. Actors Marlon Brando, Arthur Mitchell, and James Dean studied there. Dunham later developed the Performing Arts Training Center of Southern Illinois University. Through the center, she brought artists and scholars from Haiti, Brazil, and Senegal to the people of St. Louis. In 1986, she received the Distinguished Service Award of the American Anthropological Society.

Source: Women's History Project

started with the fundamentals and then had to audition to get into an intensive program where you took a certain number of classes a week. I loved it, but it was really hard and there was a lot of pressure.

"Half way through the year I also started taking classes at Murray Lewis' Alwia Nikolais Dance Lab. I was 18; I had lots of energy, and I could take two or three classes a day. That was actually fun for me."

## College Inspires Her

"Diane Gray was at the Martha Graham school during this time, and she gave me a lot of support. She also gave me some really good advice. 'Don't just dance,' she said, 'it won't be enough for you.' After a year I decided I had to go to college, so I applied to the University of Colorado in Boulder, near where my parents and I had been skiing on vacations. I thought, I can ski and study.

"Because I had studied in New York, my dance technique was so strong that I went into all the advanced dance classes. I started making up dances and took a creative writing class. I loved it. I started to write things you would say when you were dancing; then I started choreographing things where people would talk and move at the same time. That was the beginning of me seeing dance as a story in my mind. I became an English major with an emphasis on creative writing."

After graduating from college, Terry went to London for a summer to study at the London Contemporary Dance School. Then she moved to San Francisco, where an old friend offered to let her move into an apartment that was cheap, and she got a job with a publisher of tourism materials as an assistant editor. She hated it, but she took dance classes at the same time.

Credit: "Make Believe" Jeff Porter & Terry Berliner

In one of her dance classes she met a man named Jeff Porter, who became a good friend. The two of them put together a show they called Make Believe, the story of a boy and girl growing up together. They raised money to produce it, choreographed it, starred in it, and publicized it. They made about $5,000 from the show, which ran two long weekends. It was just enough to pay for the theater, the set designer, and other production expenses. "It was a great experience to collaborate with someone who had a similar vision and sense of humor."

Terry also took acting classes at the American Conservatory Theatre while she was in San Francisco. "I felt that if I was going to write for actors who danced or dancers who spoke, I needed to know what they went through. At the school I met a woman who taught the Alexander method of movement for actors, and she asked me to teach movement to her students. It was the beginning of me working with real actors."

After two years working and studying at the Conservatory, Terry decided to go to graduate school. She was accepted into the dance choreography program at University of California at Los Angeles. "The good thing about choreography is that you can make the dance whatever you want, it can embrace theater as much as you want."

Shortly before she left for graduate school, Terry met Andre, her future husband. It was love at first sight. Eventually she convinced him to come to Los Angeles, and then to San Diego, when she found a job there.

## Choreography in San Diego

After grad school, Terry got a job in San Diego with City Moves, part of the San Diego Foundation for the Performing Arts. Her job was to choreograph two complicated dance numbers for a large group—kids, parents, and grandparents—to be performed at the San Diego Convention Center. This was quite a challenge. First, Terry was working with amateur dancers who ranged in age from 5 to 60. Second, she had 40 people in a single number. Third, she had to choreograph two different numbers that would be performed on stage at the same time, which meant that she had to plan for those groups of dancers to be performing together. "There were 10 choreographers working on this show. It was a sprawling set that could accommodate 300 people, and it was like a three-ring circus, but it was so much fun to work on."

Terry loved her life in San Diego—working as a choreographer, teaching dance in the schools, and writing some original material. But when her husband was offered a job in New York, she went with him. "I thought, I'll see what I can do in New York."

## How She Got Her Foot in the Door

In New York, she saw an ad in *Backstage* magazine for an open meeting of the Society of Stage Directors and Choreographers. She decided to attend. "The meeting was filled with many people I had only read about in books, legends of the dance and theater community. I sat there and thought 'these are the people I want to know.' So when the meeting was over, I went up to the executive director of the Stage Directors and Choreographers Foundation and said, 'I want to volunteer for you. I will do whatever you want me to do, for free.' He called me not long after that and asked if I would like to work on an issue of the SDC Foundation journal. That eventually led to a paid job as associate editor."

The SDC Foundation had an observership program, to which Terry applied and was accepted. She was paid a small salary and worked as an assistant director with Susan H. Schulman. Terry gained valuable experience in directing and choreography New York style, and she still does many shows with Susan, a director who turned out to be a good friend and mentor.

**Most jobs come through networking.**

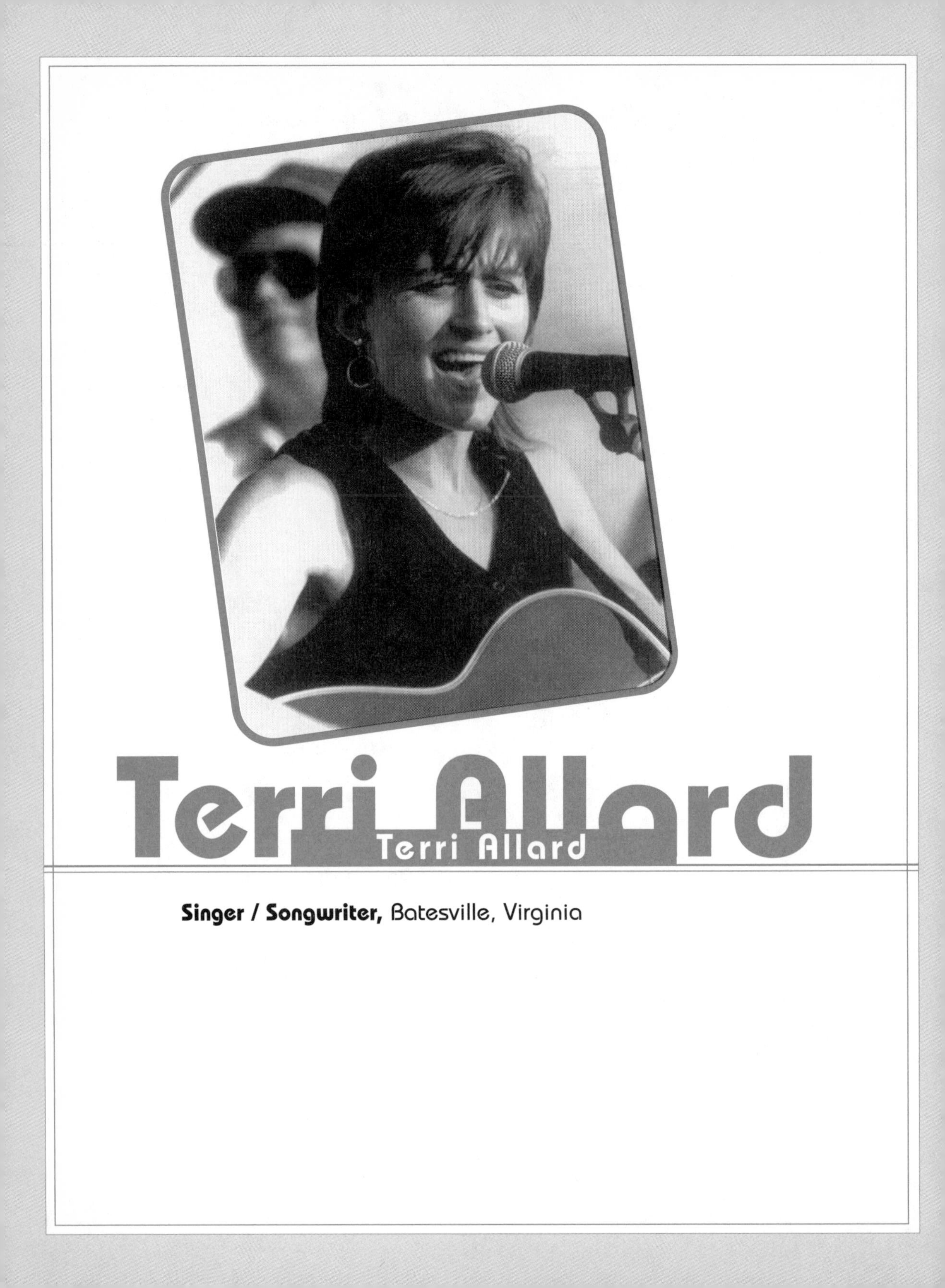

# Terri Allard

Terri Allard

**Singer / Songwriter,** Batesville, Virginia

# Singer Songwriter

## True to Her Musical Roots

Terri Allard is a songwriter and singer of immense power. Her music is evocative of the best in the American traditions of old country, folk, jazz, pop, and blues. This "roots" music fuels her, but her songs are intensely personal. Her lyrics are filled with stories of love, lust, loss, longing, and hope. Her voice is inviting; you want to know her better. (One critic described her as having a low soprano voice that sneaks up and grabs you.) "My father is a photographer with a great deal of artistic integrity. He's also very musical. My sister and brothers and I grew up with 'roots' music. I've been in love with it since I was a kid. And I learned from my dad early on to be true to myself and to stick with the music I love," Terri says.

**Singer / Songwriter Americana**
Singers/songwriters earn money from the sale of CDs and from touring. If someone else sings their songs they get royalties for record sales and radio play. Working full-time, well-known regional singer / songwriters can make from $10,000 to more than $100,000 per year after expenses.

# TERRI'S CAREER PATH

- Wins talent show at age 9
- Sings in school, bars, and for local benefits
- Leaves college after a year, waits tables, sings

It took Terri until her late 20s to focus full-time on a music career. Today, at 37, she is nationally known in this roots or—"Americana"—style of music. She tours from her country home in Batesville, near Charlottesville, Virginia, often with harmonica player Gary Green. Terri has developed a strong base of loyal listeners throughout the United States. She has recorded three CDs, on her own private record label, Reckless Abandon Music. She sells her CDs at her performances and through record stores. She also sells CDs from her Web page, (http://songs.com/terri). She has opened for Americana singer John McCutheon at the Wolf Trap Center for the Performing Arts outside Washington, DC, and played on the same stage as Peter Yarrow of Peter, Paul, and Mary. The well-known duo Robin and Linda Williams sang harmony on "We'll Have Elvis," a song about driving across the country and listening to music in the car that appears on Terri's latest CD, *Loose Change and Spare Parts*.

Terri's life is filled with making music, listening to music, and running her music business. Her husband, Dwayne Evans, is her business partner. He helps Terri market and produce her music. Terri also has an agent and a manager who get her bookings throughout the United States.

## Gigs, Songwriting, and Business

"My schedule varies. I might perform almost all month, or I may have a month where I only have four gigs, and I write music or take care of the

Takes part-time work, performs and writes music

Forms Terri and the Terrifics, takes voice lessons

Marries Dwayne, runs the business with him

business side of things. In this business, you have to make decisions about how much time to invest touring new places, where the audience does not know you. In these places you won't make much money—$50 to $100 a night. You can sell CDs that will pay your tour expenses but won't pay for your time. This type of touring is an investment to get better known with new audiences. Then when you've built your fan base, they are on your team, and you can go back to that town and play to a larger crowd and therefore make more money. The other type of touring is where you are well-known. This is the type of touring you do to earn your living. You have to balance when you are out touring as an investment and when you are out touring to people who know you so that you can pay the bills."

Credit: Jodi Sussman

Terri decided to produce and distribute CDs herself rather than "shopping" for a big name record label to represent her. "When I made my first CD in 1994, it was because the people who came to listen to me asked me if I had CDs, so I knew that I could sell

recordings. You also need a CD to send out with a promotional package to represent your music. But there is no point in having a nationally known label unless you are touring nationally. There are only about 200 radio stations that play the type of music I record and perform. So it's easy to get my CDs distributed to all the radio stations that play me. The income after the expenses of making, marketing, and distributing the CDs is ours with our own label. If I had a big name label they would take a large chunk of the sales money. The sale from my CDs are a big part of what I make. Besides, Dwayne and I like having control over the music and the distribution."

Terri's second CD, *Rough Lines*, was recorded in a two-room chapel in Charlottesville where the acoustics were wonderful. "Everybody was in a circle with their own mic and their own track. We put the accordion player in the bathroom because he was too loud. The drummer played light percussion, snare drum, and high hat, and we put him in the other room of the chapel. For three days we just played. The group had such a natural groove. I was afraid if I took it to the studio, I wouldn't be able to keep that. This was my baby, so I released it on my label. When *Loose Change and Spare Parts came out*, I just kept going with my own label. If I record another CD it might be time to shop for a nationally known label, because I am touring nationally now, and a label would help with distribution and name recognition."

Two or three times a month, Terri takes voice lessons from a classical composer and music teacher. "Edmond is wonderful. We worked up two numbers for an AIDS benefit. Doing classical duets with my music teacher was an incredible experience for so many reasons. It was a new challenge. I'd never performed like that before. My home-town got to hear me sing semi-classical music, and they were not expecting that. I came out on stage and performed some of my original music with my guitar. Then I put the guitar down and walked out toward the audience to do a song from the musical *Baby, Baby* called "What If We Had Loved Like That." It's all mid-tone to falsetto, not the range where I usually sing. I looked at the audience and they looked at me, and I thought, okay, here we go. I was baring my soul; naked out there without my guitar. But the audience loved it. And I loved the challenge. It wasn't like when I was younger, and I avoided trying new styles of music."

## Arts a Part of Life

Terri started performing in public at age nine. She was the third of four

## CAREER CHECKLIST

### You'll like this job if you ...

Love to perform

Are creative and energetic

Are well-organized and will learn the business side of music

Have musical talent

Don't need a lot of structure in your life, the music business is chaotic

Are willing to tour to different cities to establish your reputation

children born in four years. She grew up in Barboursville, Virginia, a small town in Orange County, where her family lived in an old farm house and kept a pet pig, raccoons, horses, goats, chickens, dogs, and cats. Her

Credit: William A. Allard

father is a photographer for the National Geographic and travels all over the world. Both her mother and her father love the arts, and the house was always full of interesting, "artsy" people. One time, when Terri was nine, a friend of her father's visited and brought her boyfriend, who played "Leaving On A Jet Plane" on his guitar. "I was just gone. I sang that in a 4-H talent show and won. And that's when I began to realize that not everybody was quite as musical as I was. I thought everybody sang. My sister and I had sung from the time we were born, practically. We were always putting on shows and forcing our friends to either be in them or watch."

Terri's parents helped to found the local theater group in Barboursville. "I grew up in that theater and that was a wonderful thing. You learn so much about the different aspects of performing—what it takes to put a show together, all the back-stage work that goes on. I've been the prop girl, the make-up girl, in crowd scenes on stage, and in some decent roles that didn't require a great actress. We produce our own shows now, and we do a good job. I'm sure a lot of that comes from growing up in the theater. The music business is not just about getting up and singing a song. There is a lot of organizing and production work."

In school Terri liked anything artistic. She was good at English, art, and music, but science and math were a struggle. "Later in life I had a guitar teacher who taught me music theory, and I realized how much of it is math related. I could have used music to better understand math if I'd paid more attention at an earlier age."

## A Lesson About Voice Lessons

In elementary school, Terri and her friends always asked to put on shows and sing assemblies. Terri was in the school chorus and enjoyed singing the Hallelujah Chorus from Handel's Messiah at Christmas. Her mother made sure Terri got a couple of voice lessons, but Terri was afraid of lessons. She didn't want anybody to change her sound. She liked the low, husky voice of the folk singer, and she thought if she took lessons, she would be taught to sing like an operatic soprano. Today Terri knows that lessons aren't about changing your sound. They are about singing properly and keeping your instrument in shape. "I was a distance runner in high school, and I compare taking voice lessons to warming up before a track meet. You don't run seven miles without loosening up, stretching, and taking care of your muscles first. Lessons are like that; they are to take care of your pipes."

Terri and her boyfriend Mark played and sang in local bars and restaurants for tips and small fees while they were in high school. Their parents had to go with them because they were too young to play in some places. They also played a lot of local benefits like the Lion's Club. Everyone knew Terri and Mark as performers, so when there was a need for singers, they would ask the duo to perform.

## Searching and Playing Music

Terri went to college at Mary Washington College in Fredericksburg, Virginia, for one year. It was the wrong college choice for her. She wasn't interested in her classes, and she thought the college, a mostly girls' school, was too conservative. She had chosen it because it was close to home. After a year, she decided she would go to Nashville and be a singer. She counted on having Mark go with her, but he ultimately decided he didn't want to go. So, not comfortable with the idea of going alone, Terri joined a girlfriend who was taking a year off from school to ski and wait tables at Wintergreen ski resort outside Charlottesville. Terri sang and waited tables at Wintergreen for a season.

That was the beginning of a ten-year quest to find out what she really wanted to do with her life. During this period, Terri performed part time and continued to work on her music. She took jobs to support herself. She didn't have the same drive that she has today to make her music a full-time profession. "Even though I identified 100 percent with being a singer and knew it was a very large part of who I was, I felt that if I didn't label myself that way, I wasn't responsible if I failed. Until I told myself that I had to focus on that and give it everything I had, which was in my mid 20s, I didn't feel I had to live up to anything."

**I could just kick myself for not realizing how valuable voice lessons were when I was younger.**

Terri played alone and with other musicians throughout Virginia, learning how to develop her own unique sound and to write her own songs. She played for a number of years with another musician from Orange County, Bill Brockman, who taught her to just be herself. "Why do you want to sound like somebody else?" he asked her. She and Billy formed a rockabilly band called Terri and the Terrifics. "I was singing in keys that were a hair too high for me. It was easy for the guitar player to be in a certain key at times and I would sing in the key that was better for him. That is something you should never do.

"I also was smoking, and my breathing techniques were terrible. When you sing on top of a band, you tend to sing louder and harder to get the sound out front. I developed some very bad habits. I quit smoking, because I knew that it was very bad for my voice, but shortly after that I found I was losing my voice. I went to the doctor and he discovered vocal nodes, very small calluses, on my vocal chords. These were teeny, but if they get too big you need surgery and it can be serious. The doctor told me to stop singing for three months and to immediately begin taking voice lessons. He gave me Edmond's name and told me to see him right away so that I could learn to sing properly. The fact that I couldn't sing then made it so clear to me how much singing was a part of my life. I never wanted to risk losing it again."

Terri has chosen a style of music, Americana, that probably never will push her to the top 40 charts. But she makes a living in a competitive field, exposes more people to her music every year, and gets to fill her life with music. "I would like to do well in Nashville, to have people there notice my songwriting. People often compare me to Mary Chapin Carpenter because we both write about social issues and our style is part folk, part country. I was encouraged when Nashville embraced her because she is such a talented songwriter, though not your typical top 40 female country singer. But I know how difficult it is to get noticed. I won't sing something just because it is trendy. If a country singer wants to pick up my songs and sing them in a trendy way, that would be fine, but for me, it's important to stay true to my roots."

# Susan Wall Kronenberg

Susan Wall Kronenberg

**Puppeteer and Owner,** Carousel Puppets, Sterling, VA

Major in Theater Arts

# Puppeteer

## She Pulls the Strings

The Holly Follies, one of Susan Wall's current puppet shows, is about Holly the Elf and her comic attempts to organize a talent show at the North Pole. Among the cast of Circus on Strings, a marionette variety show that Susan also offers to her customers, are a ballerina, a clown that comes apart, another clown that tosses a pole, a bunny on roller skates, a cat on the trapeze, and an opera singer. The Monster Review showcases a monster that juggles his head, a four-faced alien, and a Martian with a slinky body.

Puppeteer: Income will vary depending on the amount of marketing you do and the area of the country in which you live. A realistic expectation for a serious puppeteer is $35,000 per year or more.

Susan is the owner of Carousel Puppets in Sterling, Virginia. She creates all her own puppets and puppet shows and performs at schools, libraries, parks, summer camps, shop-

# SUSAN'S CAREER PATH

Acts in high school

Graduates college, goes to New York

Goes on tour with Nicolo Marionettes

**I like being my own boss, but sometimes I miss having other people around to work with.**

ping malls, and as entertainment for parties in the Washington, DC area. "I get work year round, but in the summer I am very busy. For example, a I did 11 shows in four days for a series of recreation centers in Maryland. The week before school starts it dies down a little and then starts back up in the late fall."

## The Making of a Puppet

Some puppeteers buy their puppets from other puppeteers, but Susan makes all her own puppets. She recently attended a two-week, intensive workshop at the University of Connecticut. Under the instruction of a German master puppeteer, Albert Roser, she learned to make and operate puppets in his unique style.

"I made one of the elves in the Holly Follies using the woodworking techniques I learned in the class. But most of my puppets are made of fabric, with paper mache for the head. I start with the head and the rest sort of flows from there. The most fun part is the painting and costuming. I love to paint the heads. I put on hair of yarn or feathers, and then I decide on the costumes. Then I have to get the strings right. It usually takes half a day to get the strings balanced so the puppet will move right. After I have used the new puppet in a performance, I may have to re-adjust the strings. I'll think, I want the puppet to move more this way or that and will either attach new strings or adjust the existing ones to make that happen."

The basic puppets have nine strings (Susan uses black nylon fishing line), but usually Susan adds more so the puppets can move better. For example, she will add strings to the back of the heel so that the puppet

# SUSAN'S CAREER PATH

Works off Broadway in a Bil Baird's production

Has Wendy and Andrew, moves to Virginia

can lift his foot. Or she will add extra strings on the hands so that the puppet can juggle balls. "Many of my puppets are traditional marionette puppets. I have a few books on marionettes that give me ideas."

"The puppets are lots of fun to make. They are a little like my children. When I've finished making them, it feels weird when someone else picks them up and operates them."

Susan has two "real" children—Wendy, 7, and Andrew, 3. She works at home and is able to arrange her schedule so that she can spend time with her kids. She has been in business for herself 15 years. For much of that time, she also did the marketing, but in the last few years her husband, Peter Kronenberg, has taken over this aspect of her business. He places advertisements in parenting magazines and creates and mails brochures to get customers like schools teachers and librarians.

"You can make a pretty good living as a puppeteer, but it's harder when you have a family. My husband is keeping his day job in computers for a while." Occasionally Susan will get a call from a potential customer at a library or county parks department to audition. If the customer likes her, that often will lead to a steady stream of work, such as the 11 shows she did recently for the recreation centers. However, most of the time people will hire her without an audition.

Susan performs most of her marionettes cabaret style—out front with the puppets, not hidden behind the curtain like many traditional puppeteers. "I show the audience how I work the puppets up front and then they can relax and just pay attention to the show." Most of her shows are geared toward children, but adults love them too. "I have one puppet that is a hula dancer, and the adults always come up and say they love the way I do that one. But then, so do the pre-schoolers."

## A Flair for Character Voices

Susan, who grew up in Rialto, California, loved theater in high school, and was in all the productions of the drama club. She majored in theater arts in college at California State University, Fullerton. When she graduated, she headed for New York City to make her living as an actress. She had friends who lived in the city, and she stayed with them until she could find her own apartment. She finally found an inexpensive apartment that was "rent stabilized" in Manhattan. She lived there 15 years. Because of the laws, the landlord could raise the rent only a small

## CAREER CHECKLIST

### You'll like this job if you ...

- Love to perform
- Know and appreciate music, have musical ability and good timing
- Like arts and crafts and don't mind getting your hands dirty
- Will learn to do different types of voices
- Love kids
- Think you could run a business
- Will learn the financial and marketing skills you need

GROUNDBREAKERS

### Pioneer Puppeteer Designs for Edgar Bergen

Puppeteer Virginia Austin Curtis (1903-1986) got her start in the puppet business in 1933 with the Olivera Street Marionettes. Three years later she designed Clippo the Clown, which she sold to California department stores and later to Marshall Field's department store in Chicago. She then opened a puppet shop, where the famous ventriloquist Edgar Bergen commissioned her to make the first head of Elmer Snerd, who later was named Mortimer Snerd.

Source: Women's History Project

amount every year, so she could afford to stay in New York. It was difficult to find paid work as an actress, although she did work off off Broadway—acting but getting paid very little. Puppetry provided a steady income.

"I went to an audition where they were looking for actors who could do character voices. I had studied voice in college. It turned out to be a small puppet company, Nicolo Marionettes, that wanted people who were strong performers. They figured they could train us how to work the puppets."

Susan had a "baptism by fire." "I was given one week's training and then sent on a road tour right away with two other people. We were given about a week to learn the basics of operating the puppet. It's like playing the piano. You can play the scales after a week but it takes much longer to be able to perform a piece well." After touring for a few months, she came back to New York, and worked in the shop, learning how to make the puppets.

Susan stayed with the company for eight years because it was steady work. Then she struck out on her own, getting work on a cruise ship performing with puppets. She also worked a few summers for the city of New York at the Cottage Marionette Theatre in Central Park. In 1990, she was offered a position off Broadway with the Bil Baird Puppet Theater, doing a production of Alice in Wonderland at the John Houseman Theater. "I got hired because I was a good puppeteer, and I could do lots of character voices. In puppet plays, you often will be asked to perform from three to eight characters, and you have to be able to do the different voices. I could also match my speaking voice to the singing voice that was recorded on the tape."

One day one of Susan's puppeteer friends who was married to a computer specialist had a party for puppeteers and computer people. Susan met Peter at that party. When they married, he moved into her studio apartment. When Susan got pregnant with her daughter Wendy, the New York apartment became too small, so the couple moved across the bridge to

a larger home in Teaneck, New Jersey. A couple of years later her husband found a job in Virginia.

"I work even more in Virginia than I did in New York," Susan says. "One of the good things about being a puppeteer is that you can go out and find your own work. It's not exactly like waiting for call-backs on auditions for acting jobs."

Susan hopes that she can continue to grow the business. Someday she would like to hire other puppeteers to work with her.

# Elaine Rendler

Elaine Rendler

**Director,** Georgetown Community Chorale, Washington, DC. Director of Music Ministry, Bellarmine Chapel / Catholic Campus Ministry, and Lecturer, George Mason University; Fairfax, VA

Major in Music Education; Master's degree in Organ Music; Doctor of Musical Arts, Catholic University of America, Washington, DC

# Choir Director and Organist

## Inspirational Music is Her Ministry

Dr. Elaine Rendler teaches and arranges music, directs a number of choirs, writes about music, and plays the organ at church events like weddings, funerals, and special celebrations. Elaine has devoted her life to church music and to musical education. "I don't do one thing brilliantly; I do lots of things pretty well," she says.

Elaine teaches music theory four days a week to students at George Mason University (GMU) in Northern Virginia. Her keyboard students are musicians who play instruments, other than the piano. She has clarinet players, flutists, French horn players, trumpeters, guitarists, and students majoring in voice. "We work through headsets, so we can play together, in a

**Music Faculty: Full-time faculty at colleges, universities, and conservatories earn up to $60,000**

Source: *Career Information Center.* (7th ed.). (1999). Macmillan

**Church Organist and Choir Directors: This is usually part-time work that pays an average of $40 to $100 per week.**

**Choral Group and Opera conductors: At the community level, this is part-time work for as little as $8,000 and up. Those in permanent positions with established companies in major cities can earn more than $100,000 per year.**

Source: *Encyclopedia of Career and Vocational Guidance.* (2000). Chicago: J. G. Ferguson.

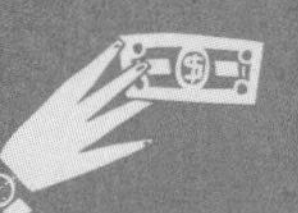

Takes piano lessons at age six

Learns organ, decides her career is choir director

Earns her way playing piano and organ

quartet, or silently to ourselves. Every musician needs to be able to play the piano at some point in her musical career."

Elaine is fond of working with students. "They are great fun and have a lot of energy." Her other jobs are director of music ministry and music director at Bellarmine Chapel, which is the Catholic chapel for GMU. "Music ministry here consists of a choir, cantors, and a variety of instrumentalists. I play for weddings and church services. My weekends are busy at church. I'm there for liturgy on Saturday at 5:30 p.m. and finish after the last Mass on Sunday night, which begins at 10:00 p.m. Almost everybody at that Mass is college age. They like to stay up really late. While the people in my keyboarding class generally are preparing for a music career, the people I work with in the chapel have many different careers in their future. Some have sung in high school choirs and some just want to sing for God and their church. Our chamber ensemble has some really good instrumentalists."

In music theory, students study the technical building blocks of music such as sight singing, ear training, and harmony. "Learning how music is put together helps you really understand the music you play."

## Started Her Own Choir

On Wednesdays, Elaine works with the Georgetown Chorale, a group of singers she started 12 years ago. "I thought maybe there were a lot of people who didn't go to church but

Graduates college, teaches music to inner city kids

Earns master's and doctorate

Teaches and has choirs at Georgetown University

wanted to sing religious music and to serve the community. We began with 8 or 10 people rehearsing in one of the high schools."

"We organized as a nonprofit organization. In the beginning, we created bylaws that said 'We are here for musical excellence and for the musical education and development of each person in the group.' We then expanded to all kinds of music. A second important point was that we were there to share what we had with those who have less than we do. When you join the group, part of the membership requirement is outreach. You can donate money, have a garage sale or a cake bake, or find donors to help support us. We've had people say to their friends and relatives, don't give me anything for Christmas. Donate the money to the Chorale. After we pay our expenses for the year, the rest goes to a charity."

**Conducting is having something to say and saying it well.**

The Georgetown Chorale, which has swelled to more than 100 singers, gives three performances a year. One is a Christmas song fest at the Kennedy Center in Washington, the other two are in the spring. The group has performed to help a church raise money for special projects such

Starts Georgetown Chorale

Teaches at George Mason U, directs chapel choir and ensemble

as handicapped ramps or a new organ. The Chorale has gained a loyal following among those who love good choir music.

On Thursdays, after teaching, Elaine has music rehearsal at the chapel. On Fridays, she travels to conduct workshops for church choirs. Saturdays when she is not out of town, she plays for weddings. Sunday is church and recreation day.

## Recording and Writing

Elaine has made several CDs, some with the Georgetown Chorale. Recently, she finished a recording, for Oregon Catholic Press, of traditional and folk church music medleys that she arranged for piano. "There are people who are strictly traditional, where the music is traditional, and those who go to 'contemporary' Masses. I started thinking that they ought to be able to relate to each other musically. When I wrote *Keyboard Praise*, I tried to blend traditional pieces with folk pieces. So you'll find tunes such as the delightful Sydney Carter tune, I Danced in the Morning, next to a beloved tune such as How Firm a Foundation."

Another CD project Elaine was recently involved in is titled *Sabbath Gate*, a recording of stories, songs, and prayers for the Jubilee year of 2000. "I didn't perform on the CD; I helped pull it together. The CD is based on the Jubilee tenets of Sabbath, justice, forgiveness, and celebration from the *Bible's* Book of Leviticus. I've also been asked to coordinate the Jubilee celebration for the Catholic diocese in Richmond,

Virginia. They are expecting 9,000 people, so I have to choose the music that would be appropriate for so many people to sing and to put together a program for the choir." Elaine also writes columns for church music directors with tips on how to direct a church choir.

"I believe everybody is equal in that we all have gifts, but not everybody's gifts are the same. One teacher in high school said to me, 'Elaine, don't take any more math. You can never do more than Algebra 2. Your brain just doesn't work that way.' I don't do everything well. There are musicians who do one thing really well, and you find them in the concert halls of the world, and there are other people who have to put together a number of things to survive, and that's what I do."

## Rewards Are Great

One of the most rewarding things about Elaine's work is that she makes a difference in the lives of so many people. "When you play music at the

## CAREER CHECKLIST

### You'll like this job if you ...

- Have discipline and will work hard
- Believe you can be a good musician
- Want to say something through music
- Love to teach others
- Don't mind being alone to practice
- Like working with people to create something beautiful
- Consider music a ministry, a way to serve God

## GROUNDBREAKERS

### Among the First Female Choral Directors

Eva Jessey (1895-?) brought the African American spirituals of rural Kansas to some of the greatest stages of the world. One of the first female choral directors, Eva Jessey gave concerts that were a complete panorama of early black American vocal styles. The daughter of a Kansas chicken picker, Jessey began to make a name for herself in the late 1920s when the Eva Jessey choir, first known as the Dixie Jubilee Singers, was heard over the radio in millions of homes. Jessey was the choral director for the original opera *Porgy and Bess*, which opened in 1935. She also was chorale director for *Hallelujah*, one of the earliest motion pictures about African American life, and for *Four Saints in Three Acts*, the first Broadway musical that used African Americans in a drama not specifically about African American life.

Throughout the mid-1960s, Jessey toured with the traveling production of *Porgy and Bess* as choral director. Jessey also composed her own music, including the folk oratorio Paradise Lost and Regained, with the music based on spirituals and a text taken entirely from Milton's epic poems of those titles. She served as guest conductor and lecturer in residence on university campuses and acted as both choral consultant and actress in feature films.

Source: Women's History Project

important events of people's lives, like weddings and funerals, people remember you. When you direct a choir, people are usually there because they want to sing with you. They like what you stand for." Elaine has had several experiences where students she had in the past show up as musicians in her present. For example, a man she taught in junior high school, in inner city Philadelphia back in the late 1960s, is now a renowned organist in the Washington area. He remembers his classes with her. Another young woman, whose mother died of cancer some years ago, had called Elaine to help prepare the funeral music. The daughter appeared recently in Elaine's life and Elaine helped her to get a start singing at the university.

Elaine is the oldest of eight brothers and sisters. She grew up in Landsdowne, Pennsylvania, and attended Catholic schools all the way through college. When she was six, the nuns came to the classroom and asked who wanted to take piano lessons. She said she did, but she did not have her mother's permission. A nun called her mother to ask if it was all right. Her mother said if she really wanted to, she should, even though with eight children her mother had to be careful about how much things cost.

**You know what sound you want to hear, and you shape the notes to get that.**

## Learns to Play the Organ

Elaine's grandmother played the piano by ear. She loved the organ and always wanted Elaine to play. One day, after Elaine had learned the piano, the music sister was sick and there was no one to play the organ for chapel. "I was told to go over to the church and prepare the music by 3:00 p.m. When you are in Catholic school you do what they tell you, so I played the organ that day. I did the best I could, and I loved it. There is a thrill to turning on the organ and hearing the wind gush through it. But the only thing the organ and piano have in common really is that they both have keyboards (some organs have four keyboards plus a pedal board). The piano is a percussion instrument, and the organ is a wind instrument.

"I continued with organ lessons. After my experience playing for chapel, they had me play more regularly, so I got the experience of playing a nice pipe organ at my parish church. When I was in high school, I took a job as an accompanist at a local high school. Once I started watching the choir director I knew what I wanted to do. The sound of people singing together fascinated me. I played the piano for the choir, and the director taught me how to do some basic conducting."

Elaine won a music scholarship to Immaculata College, just outside Philadelphia. In her music education courses, she had to learn how to play basic songs on every instrument. "We had a 90-voice women's choir (it was a women's school) that I accompanied. I learned a lot more about chorale music and directing from watching the director." Elaine also got a job during college as the organist at the Catholic Cathedral in Philadelphia.

For Elaine, college was just the beginning of formulating her ideas about music. "College is like an immersion into a great swimming pool of all kinds of ideas. Or maybe it's like coming to a great feast and getting a chance to sample all the foods."

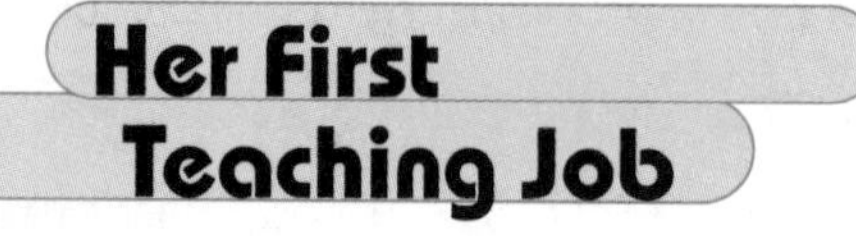

## Her First Teaching Job

After college, most people expected Elaine to teach at a private school, but Elaine had other ideas. She chose to teach at an inner city school in Philadelphia. "The principal had a special school-within-a-school program that was brilliant. Our kids did as well as the rest of the country on the standardized tests because of the way our music program worked. We put the students into music once a day in place of a major subject. For example, instead of having math five times a week, they had math four times a week and music on the other day. On another day they might not have a science class. We were feeding their souls. When good things are happening to your soul, the academics come with it. In the general music classes in the auditorium, I taught ten sections of students at one time."

When the program got cut because a new principal came to the school, Elaine decided she didn't want to stay at the school anymore. She knew that Catholic University in Washington, DC, was offering scholarships for people who could accompany performers, and she got one. She worked on a master's degree in organ and played her

way through voice lessons and opera rehearsals to pay for her tuition, room, and board. She also taught a music class at Catholic under a professor who later encouraged her to go for a doctorate. "I was studying full-time, playing for operas, at church every weekend, and loving all of it."

After she got her doctorate, Elaine worked for a year at the Naval Academy chapel as the music director. Then Georgetown University offered her a job in campus ministry and teaching. She taught music theory in the fine arts department. For the campus ministry part of her job, she had chapel choirs, including Hebrew, gospel, Protestant, and Catholic choirs, and even dance and audio-visual groups. Her title was director of liturgical arts. Once a semester or more, she and her students would go to Washington jails and have the residents there teach the students songs they knew. "This was a wonderful experience for everyone."

Now, through her work at GMU and with the Georgetown Chorale, Elaine continues to serve her community, creating those wonderful musical experiences for everyone. "I don't get up to work every day. I get up to play every day, to do my favorite things."

# Getting Started On Your Own Career Path

# Getting Started On Your Own Career Path

## What to do now

To help you prepare for a career in the performing arts, the women interviewed for this book recommend things you can do now, while still in school.

**Sherri Edelen, Stage Actress, Singer**

Get involved. Most schools have creative arts or drama departments. Audition, but if you don't get in the show, help out back stage. Local community theaters have auditions and often need kids and young adults.

Take acting classes if you can. There are summer camps where the kids get to work on a show and then they perform it the last week of camp.

Think about minoring in theater and majoring in business in college. Remember it is called show business and it's all about marketing yourself—you need to know how to do that to be successful. You also have to know how to handle your finances, because money doesn't come in regularly. You have to be motivated to keep auditioning and be seen. You learn to audition well by going to as many auditions as possible. You'll be auditioning more than working. Talent can only get you so far.

**Beth Wood, Singer / Songwriter**

One of the most important things you can do is to perform for other people. Perform as much as you can, whether it's your mom and dad or brother or sister or the school assembly. Practice being on stage.

**Nina Flyer, Cellist, Recording Artist, Instructor**

Get the right training. It's very important in this day and age when there are so many musicians and not always enough orchestras for all of them.

You must have an undying passion for music to make a career out of it. Because there are so many people showing up at auditions, you have to be totally focused on playing in an orchestra if you decide that's what you want. Not everybody can be a soloist or even an orchestra player. You have to be practical. There are some wonderful things available in music and you can find a way to make your living as a musician, but it might not be in an orchestra unless you are very good and very focused. Explore all your options. And if you don't know if you should go into music or not, you probably shouldn't.

**Susan Wall, Puppeteer**

Go to the library and check out books on puppets. Then try making your own puppets.

See as many puppet shows as you can. Don't be afraid to ask the puppeteer questions after a show. Many puppet theaters need volunteers to act as ushers, to help construct the puppets, or to work backstage to grab puppets as the puppeteer hands them off.

It's important to have an acting or theatrical background. Consider going to college to study acting and music, important skills for the puppeteer. I found that I use almost everything they taught me in my theater classes—costuming, music, voice, storytelling. Some schools even have curriculum in puppetry.

**Terry Berliner, Choreographer**

The more you know about what you want to do, the more you investigate it, the better. You have to be driven and passionate. You also have to know how to manage your money, and it really helps if you have people who can support you, sometimes emotionally, sometimes financially, like my family does.

There isn't one correct way to get to be a dancer or choreographer except that you have to love communicating a story through dance. Get to know the history of dance. Seek out books about the people who are doing it. See how those legends were made, and you will begin to imagine a career for yourself.

**Jane Beard, Screen and Stage Actress**

Make your parents take you to see as much theater as possible. But start thinking now that not everybody who acts is a star. If you want to do this because you want people to recognize you, you are looking at the wrong thing. You should want to do it because you love acting and there is nothing else you want to do.

If you love thinking of becoming another person and love thinking about how and why people do things, then acting might be for you. But you have to be able to actually get out in front of an audience and say lines and not fall over from fright. Also you have to have a really good imagination.

If you have parents who disapprove and you truly love it, you have to find people who will support you. Find an acting partner, somebody you can click with and who shares your ethic.

Study history. I took a class my first year of college, and I couldn't see how it would apply, but it's the class I use the most now. That was a class on theatrical style. I had to write six 100-page papers compiling facts on various periods of history. For example, when we got to the Greek classical period, we understood the politics, the architecture, what people were cooking, and what they were reading. We did this for every major period in history, so that we had this vocabulary of everyday life. It's a great thing to draw on now. There are so many things that could affect the character that you don't even know what to look for if you don't know the history.

**Jeanene Jarvie, Ballerina**

Learn about your body and how it moves, about coordination and music, how to count the beat and feel the rhythm. Ballet is great for anyone to try, but if you are serious about making a career out of it, you will need to work hard and give up a lot. You also should be willing to move anywhere. There are companies all over the world. Just because you don't get into one company doesn't mean there isn't a place for you. Some directors want all the dancers to look alike, so you need a certain look. Don't be discouraged if you don't have the right hair color or body. Look for another company. Check out the companies on the Internet. That will give you a good idea of what type of dances they do and what type of dancers they employ.

Try to stick to the bigger schools for lessons, and if you are serious, find a summer school when you get to be 13 or 14. Go to lots of ballet. The more you see the more you will know about the different companies. Each company has a different style—contemporary, classic, modern. At the summer programs you will be with teachers from different places and will get the experience of different types of training. Every teacher is different. You need to be flexible. You may have one teacher tell you to do something one way and another will tell you to do it another way.

There are more opportunities than there used to be for ballet, but it's still a hard profession, especially for girls and women. If you don't make it in ballet, there are still ways to dance for a living. You might also consider jazz, ballroom, or modern dancing, or dancing in the theater. Whatever you do, go with the flow and don't take yourself too seriously. Things happen for a reason; if you don't get the company you want, there may be something better for you down the road.

**Elaine Rendler, Choir Director and Organist**

Piano lessons are always good. You need to have the piano for other instruments and for voice. There is not one person I've ever met who doesn't say, I'm sorry I stopped taking piano lessons.

Study English and learn how to write. You never know what you will need later in life. When I was taking English, I said, "I'm a music major, just pass me out of this." But now I have to use it in writing my columns. English also helps if you want to compose, because you have to understand the cadence and beat of poetry before you can write the music.

You will be successful if you choose a career that honors your gifts. Listen to others to find out what those gifts are. If people tell you you are really good at something, pay attention to them. You will get a hunch about what you ought to do in life. You can have lots of good musical experiences through your church, if you are gifted that way

**Tracey Wright, Singer, Military Service**

Perform as often as you can. No matter how well you sing, you could lose it when facing an audience. Try talent shows, contests, kareoke, and offer to take solos in choirs or choruses to get stage experience.

Develop your ear. Listen to different types of music, especially jazz. Everything you've been exposed to will help you in performance.

Sing whenever and wherever you can. Take vocal lessons, join a choir or chorus. Go to college if you can. Formal training helps because competition is fierce. Learn to sight read and play a keyboard.

**Terri Allard, Singer / Songwriter**

If you want to be a singer / songwriter, the most important thing is to be true to yourself. Know why you love it and exactly what you love about it. A lot of people will offer you things that are not true to what you are. They will try to take advantage of you by saying, we love your music, just give us money and we'll make you a star. Knowing what you want to be is half the battle. You will be less vulnerable then. Many people go from one style of music to the next just to make it, but you are setting yourself up to lose if you do that.

If you want to make really big money, don't become a singer / songwriter. The chances of that happening aren't good. But if money is a big factor for the type of music you want to sing, sing a commercial style of music.

You have to be realistic about the amount of money you can make singing Americana music. You will be performing in front of from 40 to 1,000 people. That's quite different than performing to thousands, like the pop and country singers do. On the other hand, I have a career that I can continue with for a long, long time. I have a loyal fan base.

# Recommended Reading

## Reference

*How To Be Your Own Booking Agent And Save Thousands Of Dollars* by Jeri Goldstein. (1998). Charlottesville, VA: The New Music Times.

A resource and guide for performing artists that includes practical advice, books to read, and contact information on helpful organizations.

*Musician's Business and Legal Guide* by Mark Halloran.

*The Craft and Business of Songwriting* by John Braheny.

## Fiction

(These books are recommended in Best Books for Young Adult Readers, Stephen L. Calvert, Editor.)

## Acting

*Broadway Chances* (1992) and *Curtain Going Up* (1995) both by Elizabeth Starr Hill. Viking.

*Happy Endings* by Adele Geras. (1991). Harcourt.

*Nutty's Ghost* by Dean Hughes. (1993). Athenaeum.

*Stage Fright* by Gillian Linscott. (1993). St. Martin. (murder mystery)

*Come Like Shadows* by W. W. Katz. (1993). Viking. (supernatural)

## Puppetry

*Painted Devil* by Michael Bedard. (1994). Athenaeum. (fantasy)

## Music

*Kelly and Me* by Myron Levoy. (1992). HarperCollins.

*The Mozart Season* by Virginia Euwer Wolff. (1991). Holt.

*Mama, I Want To Sing* by Vy Higginson & Tonya Bolder. (1992). Scholastic.

## Other

Histories and biographies offer stories of individuals in the arts. Check the nonfiction section of your library, numbers 780s and 790s.

## General References

*Encyclopedia of Career and Vocational Guidance.* (2000). Chicago: J. G. Ferguson

*Career Information Center* (7th ed.). (1999). Macmillan.

*Peterson's Scholarships, Grants, and Prizes.* (1997). Princeton, NJ: Peterson's. web site: www.petersons.com

*The Girls' Guide to Life How to Take Charge of the Issues that Affect You* by Catherine Dee. (1997). Boston: Little, Brown & Co.
Celebrates achievements of girls and women, extensive resources

## Magazines

There are many magazines in all areas of the performing arts. Check with your library and local bookstores.

# Professional Organizations

There are many organizations and groups that serve performing artists. Here are a few to get you started. A major resource for groups is *How To Be Your Own Booking Agent And Save Thousands Of Dollars*. (See Performing Arts Reference above.)

### Actor's Equity Association

A union for actors in theater and "live" industrial productions, stage managers, directors, and choreographers.

165 West 46th St., New York, NY 10036
(212) 869-8530

### Acting Workshop On-Line

Information for beginners on acting and the acting business
Web site: www.execpc.com/~blankda/acting2.html

### American Federation of Musicians (AFM)

A musician's union. Has work rules and standardized wages, offers many benefits — health insurance, retirement fund, credit union, and free legal assistance.

1501 Broadway, Ste. 600, New York, NY 10036
(800) 762-3444
1777 North Vine St., Hollywood, CA 90028
(800) 237-0988

### American Federation of Television and Radio Artists (AFTRA)

An actor's union. Has work rules to protect actors, pays for health insurance if you work enough hours.

260 Madison Ave., New York, NY 10016
(212) 532-0800
6922 Hollywood Blvd., 8th Floor, Hollywood, CA 90028
(213) 461-8111

### American Guild of Musical Artists

A union affiliated with the AFL-CIO that represents artists in the field of opera, dance, and concert.

1727 Broadway, New York, NY 10019-5214
(212) 869-3687
Web site: www.agmanatl.com

### Chamber Music America

Supports chamber music performances.

305 Seventh Avenue, 5th Floor, New York, NY 10001-6008
212-242-2022
Web Site: www.chamber-music.org

### National Storytelling Association

Seeks to provide opportunities to learn about the art of storytelling

P.O. Box 309, Jonesborough, TN 37659
(423) 753-2171

### Puppeteers of America

Members are people of all ages interested in puppetry

5 Cricklewood Path, Pasadena, CA 91107
(818) 797-5748

### Ballard Institute and Museum of Puppetry, University of Connecticut

Home of thousands of puppets including the Frank Ballard Collection

6 Bourn Place - U-212, Storrs, CT 06269
(860) 486-4605
Web Site: www.sp.uconn.edu/-wwwsfa/bimp

### Screen Actors Guild (SAG)

Union for qualified actors who pay an initiation fee and work dues, which are deducted from the paycheck. Provides health benefits and work rules to protect actors. Two locations.

5757 Wilshire Blvd., Los Angeles, CA 90036
(213) 954-1600
1515 Broadway, New York, NY 10036
(212) 944-1030

### Women in Film and Video

Advances achievement of women in film and video. Student memberships.

P. O. Box 19272, Washington, DC 20036
(202) 232-2254

### Women's Philharmonic

An orchestra whose players are women and whose mission is to perform women's music.

44 Page Street, 604D, San Francisco, CA 94102
(415) 437-0123
Web site: www.womensphil.org

### Young Audiences, Inc.

Trains performers to present live educational programs in schools

115 East 92nd St., New York, NY 10128
(212) 831-8110
Web site: www.youngaudiences.com

### Young Concert Artists, Inc.

Holds annual auditions for classical musicians; launches careers of winners and supports them an average of three to five years.

250 West 57th St., New York, NY 10019
(212) 307-6655
Web site: www.yca.org

# How COOL Are You?!

Cool girls like to DO things, not just sit around like couch potatoes. There are many things you can get involved in now to benefit your future. Some cool girls even know what careers they want (or think they want).

Not sure what you want to do? That's fine, too… the Cool Careers series can help you explore lots of careers with a number of great, easy to use tools! Learn where to go and to whom you should talk about different careers, as well as books to read and videos to see. Then, you're on the road to cool girl success!

Written especially for girls, this new series tells what it's like today for women in all types of jobs with special emphasis on nontraditional careers for women. The upbeat and informative pages provide answers to questions you want answered, such as:

- ✔ What jobs do women find meaningful?
- ✔ What do women succeed at today?
- ✔ How did they prepare for these jobs?
- ✔ How did they find their job?
- ✔ What are their lives like?
- ✔ How do I find out more about this type of work?

Each book profiles ten women who love their work. These women had dreams, but didn't always know what they wanted to be when they grew up. Zoologist Claudia Luke knew she wanted to work outdoors and that she was interested in animals, but she didn't even know what a zoologist was, much less what they did and how you got to be one. Elizabeth Gruben was going to be a lawyer until she discovered the world of Silicon Valley computers and started her own multimedia company. Mary Beth Quinn grew up in Stowe, Vermont, where she skied competitively and taught skiing. Now she runs a ski school at a Virginia ski resort. These three women's stories appear with others in a new series of career books for young readers.

The Cool Careers for Girls series encourages career exploration and broadens girls' career horizons. It shows girls what it takes to succeed, by providing easy-to-read information about careers that young girls may not have considered because they didn't know about them. They learn from women who are in today's workplace—women who know what it takes today to get the job.